Peace That Passes Understanding:
Hope and Healing For Anxious Times
by Richard Bellows, TSSF

Westfield, Massachusetts

ISBN-13: 978-1481066754

ISBN-10: 1481066757

Dedication

This book is dedicated first to Laurel Stewart. My hope for her healing launched the prayers which turned into the conversation with God shared in the words and photographs of this book.

Along the way hope for others enriched the conversation: Andrew, Anne L., Anne S., Art, Bill, Carol, Charlotte, Deborah, Dick, Henny, Joann, Judy, Ken, Michael, Nancy, Paul, Robert, Sue, Todd, Wendy, and these people who now rest in peace: Al, Betty, Clarence, Emmett, Gladys, Goalie, Grace, Jessie, Joanne, Jodi, Lisa, Paul, Peter, and Richard.

Table of Contents

List of Poems by Richard Bellows

Acknowledgments

Thanks to Elanna Bellows for editing and publishing this book and to family and friends whose affirmation and comments encouraged me along the way, especially Laurel Stewart, Andrew Wissemann, Jodi McGuinness, her daughter Karen St. Martin, Carol Bellows, Jacob Bellows, and Danielle Bellows, my wife. Her contributions to our partnership have been invaluable, including the photograph of one of the Lakes of the Clouds found on page 34.

Thanks also to the western Massachusetts churches that exhibited some of the photographs and reflections: Christ Church Cathedral in Springfield, St. Stephen's Church in Pittsfield, St. David's Church in Feeding Hills, St. Mark's Church in East Longmeadow, and Southwick Community Episcopal Church in Southwick.

Forward I

Priest, poet, and gardener, Rick Bellows shares his unique experience and perspective, using the lens of his camera and words as windows into the heart of God. Linking his background in geology with science and natural phenomena provides a spiritual substrate for his writing. As a man with a "third eye" he sees God in the tiny particles of the created earth, as well as the vast cosmos. Some of the texts, accompanied by images, are like the Psalms – the second line or phrase an expansion of the first line or phrase: the picture extends the meaning of the text. For Rick, "seeing is a skill" provided by nature and biology, honed by grace, the true icon, the eye of God.

During the acute phase of my lymphoma, these words and images illumined an otherwise dark path with hope and a renewed faith. Such thoughtful—and at times profound—reflections on life with all its quandaries and pain, have the awesome power to bring peace and a tranquility that allows for healing of the spirit and soul. These pages offer something rich and beautiful —"the peace that passeth all understanding."

Laurel G. Stewart
Longmeadow, Massachusetts
August 2012

Forward II

Not long after my parents moved closer to me so I could help with their care, a large card arrived in the mail from their former pastor, Rick Bellows. Inside was a note that related to the beauty captured in a photograph on the front of the card. By that point my parents had difficulty reading their mail, so I would read Rick's cards aloud to them. Sometimes they would ask me to read the note again and again. We were like soldiers, cherishing each word, encouraged as we fought daily battles with their declining health. The cards kept coming. We soon had quite a collection to share with friends. We even put our favorites on a bulletin board for all to see.

Rick's cards offered us glimpses of nature's beauty and words of hope and faith. They gave us the strength we needed from God to continue on our journey. The cards were truly cherished treasures for a very difficult time leading up to and after my parents' deaths. They always hoped that Rick would put his collection together somehow for others to enjoy. I am certain that my parents are proud to have inspired Rick to share his gifts and talents with them and to share them in this book with you.

Karen McGuinness St. Martin
Norton, Massachusetts
October 2012

Come, peace from beyond.
Pass into understanding,
Ever dawning new.

Preface

To make us wise, some books set out to take us to the limit of our understanding, to stretch those limits, and maybe even to give us a glimpse beyond. In contrast, this book seeks to understand peace that passes the horizon of understanding on the way in. It's all about the direction—the peace that passes understanding is peace welcomed and received.

Being a visual person, I find the wondrous gift usually arrives wrapped in an image (or at least with a beautiful card!) to be opened, unpacked, and shared with words. Again, note the movement from beyond words, into words.

Though I aim to write without offense to open minded people of any or no faith, I write as a Christian. My words follow Jesus as the Word from beyond. The movement of God in Christ is not out of this world but in. It is not escape but rather presence. (At least that is the first movement.)

Peace does not go far on momentum. It must be fresh, never stale, ever new or renewed. Therefore I keep watch for beauty in nature. My goal is to find fresh signs of God loving us now, and to share that love so we may trust and hope.

I search for signs of presence and peace so that we ourselves may become signs of God welcomed into our lives—living evidence of grace and healing. We should not expect that evidence to look like a step back to the way it was. Neither would it be an escape. Healing is what happens in us as we experience love from beyond: progress, growth, opportunity, change…

In this light, I invite you to join me in welcoming mysteries of peace, hope, and trust into your experience and into your understanding.

Peace and all good,
Rick Bellows
November 2012

The garden at The Old Hotel in Lincoln, Vermont

Introduction

In August 2008 Laurel returned to church after what I had heard had been a difficult course of treatment for cancer. When I greeted her and wished her well, she thanked me for making a greeting card she had received from a mutual friend. I had made the card for him using a photograph of flowers from his garden. Laurel's appreciation for the card was all the encouragement I needed to send her one myself.

Soon I decided I would pray for Laurel daily, and every week or two, as a visual "Amen!" I would send a card with a photograph and note reflecting on it. I would continue this practice as long as the cards remained meaningful to us both. Quickly we found that the cards and notes blessed and inspired us. Before long we sought ways to share the blessings with others. She helped by arranging the first of many exhibits of selected photographs, with their reflections beside them, in galleries and parish halls. I also started sending the cards to others.

My photographs and reflections have opened up windows into heaven by opening windows into the world. My art has helped many people see the world in its common glory as an icon through which healing, hope, and promise flow.

As a Christian inspired by St. Francis, I see God in the world—in creation, in people, and in community. The beauty that inspired me is a gift to the world—accessible to anyone regardless of their religious faith. As St. Paul said in Romans 1:20, "Ever since the creation of the world God's eternal power and divine nature, invisible though they are, have been understood and seen through the things God has made." That means wisdom is available to all people regardless of their religion. Originally I wrote the reflections to people who already had a strong and deep Christian faith. I have not written these messages to convert anyone

I pray that these photographs and thoughts will inspire hope, deepen your faith, and help you to be well. I hope you see all that is beautiful around you, and understand any messages God intends for you written in the wonderful world.

Peace and all good,
Richard Bellows, TSSF
Westfield, Massachusetts
July 27, 2012

Peace passes understanding.

2008

"In times like this, I glimpse peace beyond my angry question, 'Why?'" There may be no answer to 'Why?', at least not one that makes sense, but there can be peace."

October 27 — Autumn Leaves and
Peace That Passes Understanding

August 18 — Is the World Upside Down?

I love to photograph reflections on smooth water. Looking at it draws me in and challenges me to figure it out. At first I find in it some comic relief: "The world upside down?" Yet I also find myself drawn by the reflection capturing how I sometimes really do feel—that everything seems upside down. Even so, it reveals a deeper truth, given away by the lily pads floating, the flowers reaching up for the sun, and the ripples emanating. These things reveal that what we see is right side up, after all. The quest to float, a reach for the light, and the impact of love rolling out as ripples, give us our bearings. Eventually they orient us toward reality, but reality can be overwhelming. If sorting out what's up and what's down is too much for you now, relax; rest in the face of the mystery, and just let the scene brighten your day.

August 25 — O God, We Sip from the River of Your Delights!

(a prayer based on Psalm 36:8)

I would like to share one of my favorite places in the world—Running Eagle Falls—where water gushes out of a hill beneath a stream. Settlers named the place Laughing Brook Falls, but Native Americans named this place after Running Eagle, a woman whose, vision quest at the falls, led her to be a warrior. Her name expressed humor—eagles running were as rare and strange in their culture as woman warriors.

This was the first place we visited in Glacier National Park, planned to cast the trip as some sort of a quest for vision in the context of a reasonable challenge. Our first day the easy hike in to Running Eagle Falls was just right to get our bodies, spirits, and senses of humor ready for the rest of the trip. That first day prepared us to expect the unexpected.

The next day, what we had thought was a three mile round trip up to a scenic point nearby turned out to be a three mile trek up 2400 feet gain in elevation, then after enjoying the view, trekking back down the same way. Surprised by the steep mileage, we were even more amazed how we managed so well. We realized our self understanding was limiting us. Those first two days were like a vision quest showing us to be stronger than we had thought, opening us up to adventures far more exciting than we had planned for the rest of our trip. We met great people, hiked thirteen miles one day, some of the hike on a glacier, and we slept in a teepee.

3

We also faced fear by backpacking into remote areas and sleeping in a tent in bear country. What was best of all? Our precautions worked—we never encountered a bear. We returned home safe and sound having faced challenges and fears without being overly limited by them. To this day, Glacier National Park is my favorite place, and it all started at Running Eagle Falls. I share this story to help you face your challenges and fears with vision that sees past limitations. Welcome surprises as opportunities, and keep your sense of humor handy, too.

View from Scenic Point

Lake fed by Grinnell Glacier

September 2 — A Healing Moment Captured and Shared

I find God's healing comes to me often through nature. Sometimes it comes in a moment, like yesterday when I saw a hummingbird flit by the cleome flowers. Sometimes it comes slowly, seeping in over time. When I first saw this butterfly I thought it would be a fleeting moment, but the monarch lingered for a while—long enough for me to photograph its nectar feast. Now the healing power can seep into my soul again and again, and I can share the picture with you so it may seep into your soul, too.

September 9 — Black-Eyed Susan in the Rain

The day began with me struggling in a glum mood. This made it challenging to express my hopes in words and a picture. Determined, I took my camera outside to capture a bit of God's grace in the rain. It didn't take long to find. One look at this weeping black eyed Susan showed me God meeting us in the struggle, assuring us that no difficulty can separate us from God's love. The rain drop on the flower inspires a prayer for eyes open to see God's grace shining brightly, especially when the challenges we face darken our outlook.

September 16 — A Blue Heron's Flight
At MacMahan Island, Maine

A couple of years ago I was kayaking around an island in Maine. Suddenly a blue heron and I surprised each other as I emerged from behind some rocks that had been hiding us from each other. As I grabbed my camera the heron flew away into a little cove. I managed to catch the serene flight just before the bird flew out of sight. I am glad I did, because this photograph has given me insights into tranquility.

The heron's flight may have appeared serene, and the picture instills peace when I view it, but not because the bird was so full of calm that peace overflowed. This flight was motivated by stress, anxiety, and fear caused by my kayaking, I marvel, therefore, at how the blue heron's flight is able to instill peace when serenity was scarce. After thinking about this for a while, some questions come to mind. Does the bird's flight instill peace because we follow the path to what the bird is seeking? Or because we tune in to what spiked in importance in the midst of anxiety and stress? Undoubtedly trajectories and importance play into it, but I find I sense peace because of the way the heron flew. The character of the flight appeared smooth and peaceful looking. Even if this is pure projection, the flight suggests we can face stress without being overwhelmed by it. The blue heron reminds us that a calm attitude can help us find the serenity we seek.

May we always have the fortitude to face our anxiety and stress, not with more anxiety and stress, but rather with calm assurance that we are headed towards peace. In this way, like the Blue Heron, we will seek peace and share it, too.

September 24 — Reaching for the Light
Cattails in Jones Pond

Early one morning at a conference center, I went for a walk by the lake. The cattails by the water's edge caught my eye. I was impressed by how they reached for the light. They motivated me to review my aspirations.

What is my goal? At what am I aiming? I once aspired to influence and convince people to open up to God's love, and to influence the institutions of our society to support and communicate that love in more effective ways.

I may still want to influence and convince others, but that outcome is less important to me. Now my goal is to experience God's beauty, capture it, and share it. And so I garden, take pictures, and make cards. I realize that I pray with a similar goal. By praying I am not out to influence or convince God. I am out to experience God, be changed by that experience, and share it so others may have a similar experience. Like the cattails, I reach for the light, point to it, and invite you to reach for it, too.

If I were to ask myself what my goal is in this book, I would be tempted to say that I aim for your healing, but I do not try to convince God you should be healed. God knows that. Instead, I hope your healing be the by-product of me successfully accomplishing my purpose: to show you God's invitation expressed in so many beautiful ways all around us, and to draw you up with me into the awesome presence of God. Healing flows from that experience.

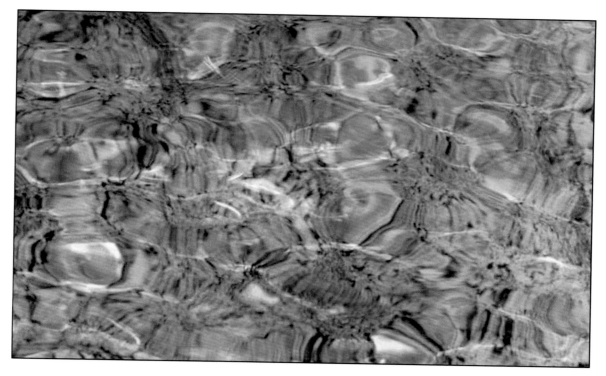

October 3 — Water and Light

A few years ago my family and I were hiking in New Hampshire on a hot day. We stopped by a cool brook, and I took this picture of the sun caught and released by the water. How refreshing! What better picture to brighten your day than a photograph of light! It reminds me of these things:

- God in us, like oil and water, an implausible mix, and yet that is what God offers.
- The promise of rainbows—light as a colorful messenger of hope.
- The waters of baptism, which capture and release the Spirit—capture and release us.
- The golden treasure we hold only by passing it on.

May the healing light of God shine in and through you.

October 3 – The Cleome

The cleome plant reminds me of fireworks. It makes me laugh.

My friend's response:
"The cleome was a true delight—wild, lively, and a thing of joy!"

October 8 — God's Invitation
"Come to me, all you who are weary and burdened,
and I will give you rest." Matthew 11:28

Looking at this picture steals the stress away. I think that is why I thought of it when I was meditating on God's invitation expressed by Jesus in Matthew 11:28. How strange, especially considering how exhausting it would be to carry a backpack through those hills! Why, then, does this picture convey rest? It certainly isn't by being colorful! The dull colors do nothing to startle; the grays and blues have a calming effect.

Yet the peace this picture evokes in me cannot be accounted for by dull color alone. Why is that? What this picture lacks in color, it makes up in depth! The view from Mount Eisenhower packs layer after layer. This illustrates the spiritual life as a trek through many layers in response to God's invitation to go in deeper and deeper. It helps me envision that inner place where God touches me with healing and life giving grace.

I pray God's healing grace may touch you deeply this week, and in as much as you are weary, I hope God brings new life.

October 14 — Oak Leaves Tell Us This Is Important

My brother visited me for the long Columbus Day weekend. He and I took our cameras to Mt. Tom State Reservation. As we hiked along the ridge overlooking Easthampton this red oak caught our eye! Like Moses drawn to the burning bush, God drew our attention and let us know, "This is important." To mark the occasion we put together a little booklet of the best of our photos, and we had a copy printed for my parents, and one for each of us. A picture of this oak is in the booklet.

The booklet and this picture represent a victory for God and a healing in our relationship. For two opinionated strong willed brothers, an artist and, well, me, to succeed at a creative project together without arguing—THAT IS A SWEET VICTORY!

It was a victory for each of us individually, but also for God who has the strongest of wills, is the most creative, and yet shows the greatest forbearance with us, creative partners such as we are. I share this picture with you knowing God wants to draw our attention and encourage us to hope for victories and healing where we face our greatest challenges.

October 21 — A Maple Leaf
So teach us to number our days, that we may apply
our hearts to wisdom. (Psalm 90:12)

I first sang Psalm 90:12 as a young man not yet a quarter century old, but the words meant a lot to me. "So teach us to number our days, that we may apply our hearts to wisdom." That is one way of expressing what I have wanted to do with my life: apply my heart to wisdom.

This very quest brings me to this time and place to consider what wisdom can be drawn from a leaf in fall. Though its days are clearly numbered, the leaf shines resplendently nonetheless. The glory it reveals remains undeterred by its imperfections. Holes and a blemish do not prevent it from reveling in the moment. The leaf inspires me to shine with humility and joy, undeterred by my inadequacies, and not needing to generate the light. It is enough to let it shine through me to be colored by my personality and attitude. So join me in seeking some sense of the number of our days that we may apply our hearts to the wisdom that inspires us to make the most of every moment and to share with others what is beautiful within us and not be hindered by our imperfections.

October 27 — Autumn Leaves and
Peace That Passes Understanding

My prayer for you this week has been overwhelmed by my prayer for another friend whose eight year old godson shot himself accidentally on Sunday with a machine gun. I kept you in my heart, but focused my prayer on my grieving friend, wondering which picture would meet me where I am in my anger and sadness, yet carry me on further? I was looking for a picture that would also lead you and my grieving friend on, too. This picture is it, with the light beyond the leaves accentuating the leaves' edge. Does it represent the edge of death that cuts off life?

The scene made me think, but the picture's balance was off without words. I could find no words that rang true until I realized what I was looking for: peace that passes understanding. I wrote to my friend, the godfather, "In times like this, I glimpse peace beyond my angry question, 'Why?'" There may be no answer to 'Why?', at least not one that makes sense, but there can be peace."

Then I realized this is exactly what I need to hear; it is exactly what I need to say. I shared it with my grieving friend to point him towards peace, and now with you to point you towards peace, too. May the peace of God which passes understanding be with you this day and forevermore.

November 6 — Focus on Delight

Today I would like to forget the darkness and focus on the light. Surely these colorful trees looking so bold and happy could shift my focus to a purely positive perspective. As the shift begins, I am aware of how we usually understand the positive in contrast to the negative, the light in contrast to the dark. Even in the Bible, the happy, those who are described as the "blessed", are usually caught up in very dark unhappy situations.

- Happy are they who escape unhappiness by taking refuge in the Lord (as in Psalms 2:12 or 34:8). Yes, but I want to focus on joy that is not defined by its contrast to the misery we seek to leave behind!

- Happy are they whom God disciplines (as in Psalm 9:12). True, but I hate to be disciplined. Even if it is good for me, I don't delight in it!

- Happiness belongs to those who fight for justice and offer happiness to others (as in Psalm 106:3 and Proverbs 14:21). Yes, but today let's not focus on the never ending struggle with darkness. Let's look beyond the hunger, mourning, and conflict faced by the blessed in the Beatitudes.

Jesus once highlighted the importance of focusing on the positive. He explained that God would heal his followers if they could see what they truly longed to see, but they looked out through calloused hearts. Blind to the kingdom of God, they did not turn to the Lord in such a way as to be healed (Matthew 13:13-16). The inability to focus on the positive blocked the healing.

We long for happy joy. Today as we turn in our quest for health and happiness, let us focus on the delight we long for, and find it healing.

November 10 — Share to Build and Build

In the shoulder between Mount Washington and Mount Monroe a hiker would pass a couple of little ponds. Up there so high, these ponds are elevated to the status of lakes, and not just any lakes, these are honored as Lakes of the Clouds. Having to work so hard to hike up to them adds to their majesty. Last July I felt honored to see them, and even swim in one of them. It was particularly wonderful to see them in the changing light, especially when the sunset reflected in the water.

As I gazed upon this scene I realized the beauty of the lake does not belong fully to the lake; the clouds lend their color and shape. Furthermore, the beauty of the clouds is not fully in the clouds; they borrow light from the sun. The lake, the clouds, and the sun shared their beauty with each other, allowing my wife and me to enjoy the scene. We passed a camera back and forth so we could offer it to you. Amazing! As we continue the sharing, the beauty doesn't diminish; it builds and builds. Now it's your turn to share it, too.

November 18 — A Funny Inkblot

Is this a panda bear with a moustache? Yes, but it's also a picture of very calm water reflecting the rock wall's markings. I took it while kayaking in Maine in 2006. It is like a Rorschach inkblot test used by psychologists to assess a person's state of mind.

They say that all the meaning we see in the inkblot is projected by us onto it. In some sense, what we see is a projection of ourselves. They say there is no objective meaning in the inkblot. Some make this claim for all of creation. I look at creation and perceive meaning everywhere. That is why I take pictures! Is this perceived meaning a projection? If so, whose projection is it?

I see meaning everywhere because I believe God is looking at creation and loving it. I hear God calling it, first and foremost, very good. Tuning in to what God sees in it, I become all the more aware of the beauty of creation, which gives me a glimpse into the mind of God. Beauty is a sign of the meaning projected by God into the world. While some would claim that the meaning I see in creation is my projection, I believe the meaning has always been from God. Before reality could ever be our inkblot, it is God's, and God's projection, not ours, makes the inkblot truly meaningful. Otherwise it would only be an inkblot.

While reality is God's inkblot, it is also ours. If we want to perceive God in it, then we had better not be blinded by our own projection of meaning into it. Our projection had better resonate with God's. For this to happen, God's projection of meaning has to find a home in us before we can see it anywhere. This is what faith is: God's meaning finding a home in us so we can see it out there.

There is a wonderful symmetry between God and us humans. We both project into reality the meaning that can be found in it. But this picture reminds me that while the wall and its reflection are symmetrical, one is only the image of the other. Like us, God projects meaning into the inkblot, but unlike us, God is the source of it all.

Wow! This silly picture has helped me reflect on serious ideas. While I have tried to speak the truth about reality in a fresh way, I take no credit for these ideas, for God inspired them through my experience in the world, confirming what God inspired through my reading of the Bible. Whether through experience or the Bible, the inspiration is through the Holy Spirit, God's projection specialist. The Spirit's projections in our lives or on the pages of a book, always express God's love. All expressions of God's love are iterations of God's chief projection given in the Son, the Word through whom all was made. Here we have all meaning summed up in an image and its reflection that looks like an inkblot. That's some projection! Wow!

November 25—Thankful for the Harvest

One of the many surprises I have found in the Bible is particularly relevant to Thanksgiving. As we celebrate the harvest, consider James 3:18: "And a harvest of righteousness is sown in peace." I would expect the order would be the other way around, that we get peace when we sow righteousness. I think of peace as a goal, but God wants me to think of it as something to start with: seed or soil.

I give thanks this week for the surprises which inspire us. I give thanks for peace, such as the peace evoked by this serene scene. I share it with you to help you reap a happy, healthy harvest from the peace that God sows deep down in your heart.

November 25 — Safe Travel

I wish you safe and happy traveling this Thanksgiving week. (Can you hear this blue heron cry, "I'm glad I'm not a turkey" ? Neither can I, but it is fun to imagine!)

December 1 — Advent Dawn

Yesterday, the first day of Advent, I woke up thinking it must be six in the morning, only to find out it was only two. The rest of the night, if I slept again, it wasn't for long. Finally at ten of six I had lain there enough. I got up, put on my boots and coat, grabbed my camera, and went outside to try to photograph stars. It was too dark to take good photographs without a tripod, but soon I focused on the dawn, and I was taking real Advent pictures.

A few hours later we went to church where a friend was the rector. As my friend preached he began with the theme, "Stay Awake!" Little did he know that experts were visiting that day. With my difficulties sleeping that morning, I was well practiced and considered volunteering to be a visual aid.

Awake and alert we were. Few people are more watchful than visitors in a church, and we were visiting. The first thing we noticed was a cool blonde Jesus shown in a perfect surfing position with arms outstretched for balance, and feet spread for stability. We laughed because he wasn't on a board on a wave in the water; he was preaching on a rock in the Sermon on the Mount depicted in a stained glass window. We found his body position funny and strange, almost as inexplicable as the practice of making Jesus look like a northern European blonde.

As we entered the nave, the large room where people gather to worship, we noticed four blue candles in the Advent wreath. My kids complained. We are used to a pink and three purple candles. In my mind I answered their complaint with gratitude for the pink and purple sky in the picture. I also thought about how the older I get, the less critical I become, at least about such things as a pink candle. I prefer to store up my critical reserves for politicians, telemarketers, and window designers who show Jesus as fair-skinned and fair-haired, surfing down a mountain.

Later that day we went with our friends to a candle shop to buy candles for our wreathes at our own homes. Our friends bought blue—for Advent. We bought purple with one pink—for Advent. I smiled, thinking of the richness of symbols, and remembering God's gift to me that morning, the pink and purple, gently fading to blue Advent dawn. I received that gift because I was awake.

December 11—Wondering about Holly

The holly bush in my parents' garden collected the frost around the outside of its leaves, making the plant look variegated. This beautiful and strange sight made me wonder if this pattern somehow helped the plant. Does it somehow spare the center of the leaf from being damaged by the cold?

The internet did not provide me with any answers. Instead, it led me to the site of a blind scientist, Geerat Vermeij, a professor at the University of California at Davis. He uses the holly leaf to illustrate how wondering is at the heart of science. He wanted to figure out why holly is prickly, and why it is asymmetrical. The left edges of the leaves often have more points than the right edges. He uses his experiences with holly to emphasize the importance of life experiences in science because they present us opportunities to be curious about what we encounter.

Wondering about experience may be at the heart of science, but it is also at the heart of faith. Worship involves awe rooted in wonder. My favorite

23

Sunday School curriculum recognized this, including a section each week to encourage children to wonder in age appropriate ways. Wondering was seen as a skill to be developed. Students were encouraged to ask questions with no definitive answer, and teachers modeled how questions about Bible stories can help us develop a sense of mystery and open us to experience awe.

As I think about the Christmas story, my curiosity abounds. How did Jesus feel when his parents talked at the dinner table about those pre-birth and early childhood stories—stories like the one about Auntie Elizabeth feeling John jump when mom greeted her, or how that old man, Simeon, came up to Joseph, Mary, and their baby as they entered the temple for the presentation, and told them that now he was free to die. Imagine the pride and confidence these stories would have inspired, but also imagine the pressure. Would these stories help a boy develop humility? If not, then how did he become so humble? Considering questions sparked by the stories, and imagining possible answers, draw me closer to Jesus.

The stories about Jesus as a child remind me of ones my parents told me, and ones I tell my children: stories of experiences that suggest how special we and our children are, and yet how ordinary, too.

Opening the stories in these ways helps me appreciate how similar he and I are in many ways, without compromising my amazement at how different we are, too (as when I consider how he turned water into wine). This approach to the Bible helps me appreciate the symmetry between me and God, and the lack of it.

I believe questions about symmetry are at the heart of both faith and science. How are these similar? How are they different? Is the universe symmetrical or not? These are the fundamental questions a physicist considers in the quest for a unified theory of everything. We long for the perfect balance of symmetry, yet we appreciate the apparent asymmetry between the amount of matter and antimatter. Given that the two annihilate each other, the universe might no longer exist if there were perfect symmetry.

As scientists debate their theories of symmetry, so do people of faith. Are we the image of God or not? Anglicans tend to emphasize the symmetry, Evangelicals emphasize the not.

One of the most amazing things about Christmas is that the Son of God gave up access to all the answers in order to take on life. Life is at its best when experiences evoke a sense of wonder. Of what benefit is it for God to experience a wet diaper? Or the prickly hay in the manger? I wonder…. and so it is all the more amazing.

December 18 — Wisdom to be Drawn by Signs of Hope

"When they saw the star, they rejoiced with exceeding great joy." Matthew 2:10

This picture of a day lily has been drawing my attention for a couple of weeks, but I kept thinking, "Not until we're closer to Epiphany!" Twelve days after Christmas, on Epiphany, we celebrate the visit of the wise people to the baby Jesus. Here I am, a week before Christmas, and I can wait no longer. What the wise travelers following their star have to teach me I find more helpful on this side of Christmas.

My hope is that we can be like those sages of long ago whose wisdom allowed them to experience God in fresh ways. These magi were not drawn to Jesus because they were the right religion; they were drawn because they were alert. Their wisdom was based on their sensitivity to signs of hope written in the universe. They were alert to creation itself.

That sensitivity is what I practice as a gardener, a scientist, a parent, a husband, and a person of faith. It is also what we practice when we reflect on these pictures of nature—seeking signs of hope in creation. This sensitivity can be developed. Seeing is a skill.

I believe God's grace can work powerfully through our sensitivity to signs of hope around us, and this can be very healing. As we prepare to celebrate the birth of Christ—God's greatest sign of hope—may we stay alert to the many hopeful signs around us, and may we find God's healing grace working in and through us.

December 26 — Gift after Gift

Do you ever have questions for God? Like, "What is God going to throw at me next?" Even if God were not the one doing the throwing, I would have wanted to ask why God allows bad things to happen. If I were God I wouldn't allow them. I am tempted to think God wouldn't either if God saw things from my perspective. And so I wonder about God's point of view, "Is there a perspective from which it all makes sense?"

I do believe there is just such a vantage point. From that perfect position God sees the blessings and knows they are worth the pain and suffering that must be endured to reap those blessings.

In high school I first read *A Question,* a poem by Robert Frost in which a voice, presumably belonging to God, asks if life is worth it. I have always thought that the answer, "It is worth it," is given in the fact that there is a voice out there asking us. I also really appreciate that the voice asks with a clear understanding of the suffering endured by both the soul and body. Life must be worth it if there is a God that truly understands the question, and God truly understands the question if God has gotten to the point of wanting to ask it. Life is worth it because God identifies with us and understands our questions.

How wrong I was to think that if God sees things from my perspective, God would not allow suffering. God does see things from my perspective. But God also sees things from God's own point of view. With that broader eternal outlook God knows life is overwhelmingly good and worth it.

Therefore the problem is not that God doesn't see things from my point of view. It's that I don't see things from God's point of view. God wants to hear my opinion. God invites me to talk about it in prayer. But God also expects me to listen and look for the broader eternal perspective. Scripture, tradition, reason, and all other revelations help me glimpse God's perspective. Creation itself is one such revelation, or rather series of revelations. Even the balloon flowers in my sister's garden give me a glimpse of God's perspective. I see one of them as a gift which has been opened.

Because the photograph is taken from just the right perspective, I see behind it more gifts to be unwrapped, reminding me of Christmas. But I see in the flowers even more: I see reality: one surprise after another. I see us—for each of us is surprise after surprise as we emerge and unfold. I see God, also one surprise after another, as we realize time and time again that God isn't exactly who or what we thought God to be. The balloon flowers brighten my day because they point me towards God's perspective which sees everything as gift after gift, each to be unwrapped in the fullness of time.

December 31 — Character and Hope

What first fascinated me about this view from the trail on a hike in the White Mountains last summer, was the silhouette of the Christmas trees. At least they are Christmas trees when viewed through the lens of the season of Christmas! Actually they are trees beaten back by the harsh mountain weather. Their struggle for light and life give them each a unique character revealed in the twists and turns they take as they reach high. They look like they are dancing with each other and the heavens.

What Christmas gift will we find hidden beneath their branches? Perhaps it is the message of Romans 5:3-5. "Suffering produces endurance, endurance produces character, and character produces hope, and hope does not disappoint us because God's love has been poured into our hearts..." I say, "Enough already with the suffering!" But I'll take all the love and hope I can get! And I'll share it with you as the sun sets on the year behind us and the new year begins. I hope this coming year will be full of hope and love for you.

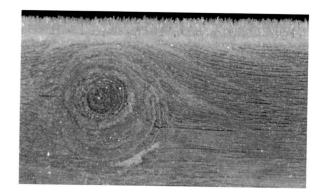

2009

"It's amazing how
Seeking beauty
Changes everything."

November 23 — Camera Eye

January 8 — Let the Sun Shine Through

This week the serious news of some friends' health struggles reminded me that praying for healing is serious business. Yet, I have also felt that God and I wanted to bring a certain kind of playfulness to the task. So I took my camera outside and took pictures of what struck a joyful chord in me. The trees cast beautiful shadows on the crust of snow, delighting my eye. My front walkway was strewn with shattered sheathes of ice that had fallen from branches as the day warmed. Both of these scenes may make the cover of future cards, but today I want to brighten your day with an image of the sun shining through. What a perfect image for the serious business of praying for healing.

January 16—Laurel's response

When I looked again at the card and message of last week...the following came: Looking up, seeing light dancing through the dark boughs reminds me of choices I've had and made. Scared by cancer, I remember it was a dark and shameful secret in my father's time. Naming it now disabled its electrifying force and brought friends. And a new peace.

January 17 — Frost

During this bitter cold week I share the frost I found on my window this morning. The crystals reminded me of a forest; or was it trees? In either event, I lived out the adage, "You can't see the forest through the trees." As I was focusing on the frost, I was missing two deer in the woods behind my house. I missed them, that is, until I looked up.

The sharp angularity of the frost makes me think of truth. Sometimes it has to be sharp to get to the heart of the matter. And I think of giant redwoods or the cedars of Lebanon. Such small things as crystals on my window can make me think big!

I'm not sure what to make of all this, but I find the frost beautiful, and therefore it gives me hope and peace. If such beauty is hidden in the bitter cold, we and our world are in good hands.

January 19 — I've Been to the Mountaintop

The Rev. Dr. Martin Luther King ended his last sermon by facing reality with hope. "Well, I don't know what will happen now. We've got some difficult days ahead. But it doesn't matter with me now. Because I've been to the mountaintop…and I've looked over. And I've seen the promised land. I may not get there with you. But I want you to know tonight, that we, as a people will get to the promised land. And I'm happy, tonight. I'm not worried about a thing. I'm not fearing any man. Mine eyes have seen the glory of the coming of the Lord."

As I was praying for your healing today, thoughts of Dr. King merged with love and concern for you. Whatever difficult days lie ahead, I prayed that God grant you courage, freedom, opportunities, and possibilities. I thought, God take my friend to the mountaintop and show her promised lands. That's when I knew which photograph I would use as a visual expression of the prayer—one I took on a mountaintop in Montana nearly 30 years ago as a geologist prospecting for molybdenum.

On this sunny mountaintop, I was struck by the sense of depth conveyed by the surrounding mountains obscuring the view of mountains beyond, which obscured the view of mountains beyond…. I found this layered view wonderful—as beautiful for what it hides as for what it reveals. And then, halfway through lunch, I finally noticed the flowers at my feet. I was surprised that the distant mountains had obscured my view of what was before me in plain sight. With such allure, can our view of the distance be trusted?

Dr. King became a visionary by seeing the glory of the coming of the Lord right up close. This glimpse of God's glory lifted his sights high enough to see the promises hidden beyond the horizon. That empowered him to look for and find signs of his dream unfolding around him.

We need enough of a look at God's glory in our midst, that we always are prepared to envision that glory fulfilled. This is especially true when the ugliness around us makes us lose sight of our dream. I take pictures to enhance our view of the glory, and to store it up. Whenever anything threatens our dream, my pictures inspire vision and assure us that there will never be a horizon beyond which we cannot hope.

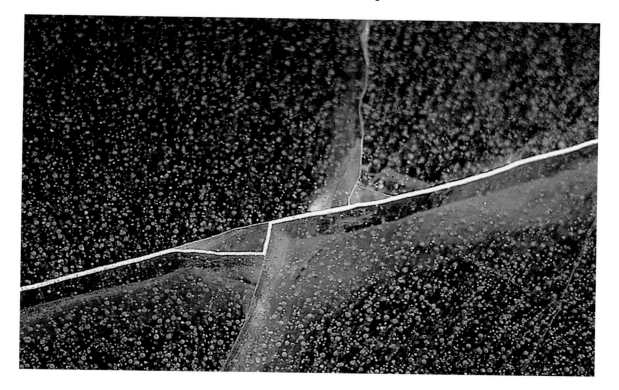

January 27—The Thin Place

In Celtic spirituality, a thin place is where the barrier between heaven and earth is thin. The term describes naturally mystical places where people tend to sense the presence of God, but also places where many prayers have worn the barrier thin. It would be wonderful if we all dwelt in thin places often, especially if we were aware. One of the goals of my photography is to suggest that thin places are all around us. The challenge is to tune our eyes to see them.

In this picture I share one of those thin places where it is easy to sense God is with us. With the sky above and the reflection on the upper of the two Lakes of the Clouds (a short jaunt down from the top of Mount Washington in New Hampshire), the land seems suspended in air. Just looking at it, my spirit is lifted as the burdens I bear lose their power to weigh me down.

I sense in the picture an invitation across the crystal sea to a place of pure presence, unimaginable access to God. The way there is narrow, just wide enough for God to draw me if I bare my soul, am stripped of all heavy defenses, and hand all burdens over to the heavenly host. I sense God welcoming me—the true me as I really am—brought into the cleansing, healing, life giving presence.

Because my love and hope for you are expressions of who I truly am, I have in some way brought you with me into this presence. While I trust God blesses you through this mystical prayer of mine, I bring you this good news: you can experience God for yourself. Perhaps this photograph will inspire you. Perhaps it will help you find a thin place around you. Consider this to be God's invitation to you, too.

February 4—A Bank of Joy

This week I expected that we would be able to escape winter with a preview of spring flowers, but the shadows across the snow bank lured me outside this morning with camera in hand. We will have to wait a bit longer for a foreshadowing of spring. The wisps of snow remind me of the perfect view of clouds in the valleys as seen from a clear mountaintop. The way the light falls on the snow also reminds me of frosting on a cake. The sweetest thing about frosting (and that is saying a lot) is that the goodness isn't superficial. It goes all the way through. How deep does goodness go in our lives?

This snow bank was good from start to finish because while shoveling to build it I had an insight: Joy is in the eye of the beholder, as long as the beholder looks at life through a lens shaped by joy. This epiphany came just in time to inspire a poem for a local contest. I share it with you, not because it is great, but to encourage you to let past joys shape how you experience life now.

In the Eye

Some say joy is an experience,
Fleeting and brief.
Others say it is a memory,
But memories fade.
I say joy is in the eye
Seeing the driveway full of snow
Through a lens shaped by the experience
Of the boy flapping his wings
And leaving in snow on the hillside
Signs he flew with a flock of angels.
The man forgot this flight of fancy,
But he wields the shovel with joy,
Always ready to fly again.

February 9 — The Eyes of April Looking Back at Us

I really look forward to spring. Given how in this picture the crocus leaves look like eyebrows, and the flowers look like eyes, I think spring is looking back for us. At least my garden seems to be looking back at me with longing eyes! These eyes make me laugh. I call it the Eyes of April because the flowers help us see beyond the foreboding ides of March, and at this point, the ides of February, too.

The early twentieth century philosopher, Ludwig Wittgenstein, reflecting on the difference between the worlds of the happy person and the unhappy person, wrote, "Eternal life belongs to those who live in the present." I consider every moment a gift, including all of winter, even shoveling my driveway. Does this looking forward to spring mean that I am not living in the present? No! I am merely enriching the present with anticipation.

Christian faith claims that it offers eternal life. Faith must therefore set us free to live in the present. That is of course its specialty! Faith is about forgiveness which delivers us from the burdens of the past and saves us from future doom and gloom.

Our faith offers us stories—both from our own experience and from our tradition and Scripture. These stories bring the past into the present in a way that expands our vision of the possibilities now. Contrast that to nostalgia, a way of looking at the past from a shrinking "Now." Worry similarly looks to the future from a shriveled present. Thank God for giving us prayer, prophecy, and promises. These orient us to the future so that hope—not worry—shapes every moment we live by stretching the limits of life in the present.

When I started writing this card, the philosopher and theologian in me were nowhere to be found, but they didn't remain hidden very long. When I delve into philosophy and theology my words can be confusing, but my prayer remains simple: May the Eyes of April looking back at you make you laugh with joy. May they help you live in the moment of expanding possibilities. In other words, may you live with hope that is hopeful enough to bless you right now.

February 19 — Flat Reality Not the Fittest

These icicles remind me of teeth, as if I were in the mouth of a dinosaur, in the struggle for the survival of the fittest. But I did not select this picture because one or the other of us is about to be devoured. Life may feel like that sometimes. It may even be useful to think that way at times; it may help us survive. So why did I choose this picture? The light shining through the icicles fascinates me, especially how it reveals their depth. You can see they are not flat because the light refracts as it enters the uneven round surfaces and reflects within the icicles.

The picture reminds me of this often forgotten insight: the world is not flat. If you look at a flat table top from above, you can see the whole thing. But to see the whole surface of a ball, or cylinder, or complex cone like these icicles, one must move the shape around, or move oneself around, to look at it from different perspectives. In the wake of the 200th anniversary of the birth of Charles Darwin, I think how some people of faith and some scientists flatten reality so they can look at it as a table top. They both make the same philosophical mistake defending their point of view as the only valid perspective from which all of reality can be seen, understood, and judged. They refuse to notice the distortions they cause in their view when they look at the world from only that one angle.

I pray for your healing, and believe God works somehow in that prayer, but I do not think that you would honor God more by ignoring all the other approaches to healing. There are doctors, therapists, nurses, medications, diet, exercise, connections with loved ones and friends, and one of the most important of all, laughter. So look at life in the rich light and laugh. Look at

40

it in the light that shines into life and reveals depths and dimensions beyond the flat surface.

I laugh to think a picture of icicles can support the healing process. Even if I look at them and see monster teeth about to devour me, I laugh, especially since I know the "teeth" have now melted. Sometimes it helps to look at scary things from different angles in time. God specializes in that—looking at our struggles from the eternal context where one can see life's difficulties have melted away.

February 28 — Twists and Turns

The leaves of the aster from last fall, dried by the winter wind, reminded me of the twists and turns of life. This was all the more poignant as I finished designing the card when my neighbor, David, came by and asked to speak to me. I welcomed him into my living room, and he then told me a sad story. His partner, Van, who had been diagnosed with cancer in early February, had just been told that his cancer could not be treated. Sometimes those twists and turns are not very beautiful.

March 10 — The Future Fed By Seasons Past

My neighbor Van died yesterday. His partner, David sent their large circle of friends regular updates via the internet. David told us about the difficulties and challenges, but also about beautiful moments he and Van shared as Van's death approached. For example David described a conversation he had with Van after Van was no longer able to speak. Van responded to questions by blinking his eyes, and these two men were able to communicate one final time their sadness, love, and humor. My lilac bush captured some of the mixture of feelings. How sad to see it so sparse, stuck in the snow. Yet how wonderful to see buds, each fed by seasons past, for a future full of life. David and Van had a history with stories and love that brightened their most difficult days, a history David and his friends can continue to tap into. Meanwhile I commend Van to God, who in the past invested everything upon a tree, to become a bud full of life for us all. May we all ultimately find our future fed by God's past.

March 12 — A Breakthrough

I anxiously await spring. My weeping pussy willow tree offered me this hopeful sign spring is on the way—the bud bursting its shell. What a breakthrough! It is such signs that bring joy to those of us who like all four seasons. It's that fifth one that's the greatest challenge: mud season. Don't get stuck in the mud. If it threatens to bog you down, remember what they say, "The only way out is through." The bursting bud reminds me of another in-between time—the teenage years. As the parent of two I relish the breakthroughs—the moments life bursts its seams, (though those moments certainly have their challenges). We all face transitions, the ending of one season and the beginning of others. Those times can be most difficult, but they offer the greatest possibility for breakthroughs.

March 22 — Ushers' Prayer

The first of these crocuses flowered by St. Patrick's day, a couple of weeks before the first ones flowered last year. I was glad to see such beautiful flowers usher in spring. When I took the pictures yesterday, these flowers were open to the sun. Today being colder, they are shut up like folded hands. Are they joining me in praying for warmer weather?

March 29 — Hope Thrives in a Fog

There is an elusive beauty to morning fog—at least it is elusive when one is trying to capture it in a picture and put it on a card! Several prototypes looked out of focus, as if I had taken my glasses off—myopic and astigmatic, but I kept trying because its beauty was compelling. So what about fog is beautiful? After all, it is usually clarity that we seek.

There is definitely something in us—one could even call it a hidden wisdom—that knows it is best to leave certain details hidden from view. I think of the pains of childbirth or the death of a loved one. If certain pains in our future were not hidden from us, we could be paralyzed by worry and fear. Instead we can be optimistic.

Hope thrives in a fog. Is this because the fog obscures tomorrow's pains? Partly yes, but I prefer to understand it thrives because the fog diffuses the light. It bends the light around the difficulties.

Whenever I have heard Jesus say, "I am the light of the world," I pictured light shining bright rays piercing the darkness. Now I add this picture: Jesus is the light that is diffused throughout the whole view. He shines so there is no dark shadow. He is the light in the fog that bends around whatever threatens to darken our day.

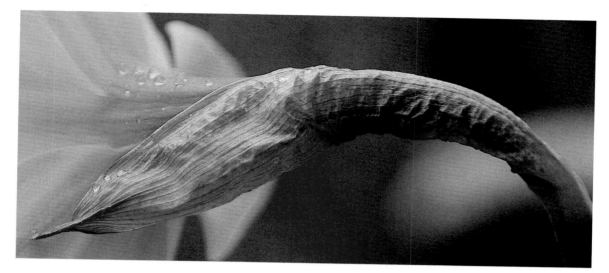

April 3 — Wonderful Transformations

When I looked out my window and saw the first daffodils had opened up, I headed out with my camera. I was struck by the back side of the flower—how it pointed the way. We all could use such backup now and again. After the example of the Orthodox who emphasize their liturgy over preaching, I thought I would allow the pictures to do the talking today, as there are such wonderful transformations occurring!

Pulmonaria   Hyacinth Bud   Pussy Willow Tree

April 10 — Sipping Bee

Twenty seven centuries ago Isaiah noticed signs in nature of God's love and care for us. "The wild animals honor me...because I provide water in the desert and streams in the wasteland, to give drink to my people..." (Isaiah 43:20). What I find surprising about this verse, is not that the animals honor God for providing for them, but they honor God for providing for us! Can we be as generous?

This bee drinking nectar at a crocus this morning reminds me of the drama remembered by the Church these days leading up to, and including Easter. In the light of Maundy Thursday, the bee sipping from the golden chalice of the crocus makes me think of the cup Jesus offered at the Last Supper. Could the bee, busy collecting pollen so that honey will flow, be a symbol of promise? Indeed, through Jesus' grail God's promises flow.

In the light of Good Friday, the scene reminds me of Jesus who used the image of drinking from the cup as facing what he had to face—he loved life, but would drink the cup poured for him: "My Father, if it is not possible for this cup to be taken away unless I drink it, may your will be done." (Matthew 26:42) Could the bee be a symbol of these words from the Lord's Prayer, "Thy will be done?"

In the light of Easter, I am reminded of the spring of the water of life offered at the end of time: "To him who is thirsty I will give to drink without cost from the spring of the water of life." (Revelation 21:6) Could the bee remind us that ultimately our thirst will be quenched? As it drinks for free, so will we!

My hope is that the bee and crocus will help you sense God present in the world, and all the more present in your life. And I hope this presence is healing for you.

April 17 — Controlling Perception

A few years ago as I stood looking across Canyon de Chelley, I saw in the distant cliff a face of a woman. Or it could be a child's face. If I push my imagination, I can see a man's face. We sure have a lot of control over what we perceive. I am reminded of the early 20th century discovery by physicists that we could decide whether light is a wave or a particle by how we look at it. We obviously have some control over what we perceive.

All this came to mind yesterday when a friend asked how I heard these words of Jesus, "If you forgive the sins of any, they are forgiven them; if you retain the sins of any they are retained" (John 20:23). I think Jesus is telling us we sure have a lot of control over what we forgive!

Whether I choose to see a woman's face, or that of a child or man, will not change the cliff. However, if I choose to see light as a photon, it does affect reality—I can't also evaluate that light as a wave. Does our forgiveness change only our minds (or hearts, or souls), or does forgiveness change reality? I believe it can change heaven and earth! At the very least, it can affect our health and happiness.

Given that our forgiveness can affect so much that is so important to us, why don't we focus more on forgiving? Why don't doctors encourage us to forgive? I find leaders of religious institutions most often horde the authority to forgive, or otherwise encourage people to retain sins rather than forgive them. Thus many religious people judge themselves and others harshly. How sad and sickening!

I don't know that forgiving will cure us of our diseases. But I do believe forgiving will make us healthier and happier. I encourage us all to hear Jesus speaking to us all. "You sure have a lot of control over what you choose to perceive as forgiven. And what you choose to perceive really affects you and the universe. Forgive: yourself and others." That's what he told his disciples on the night of the first Easter, and through them he is telling us. I believe he can really help us do that. He can help us change heaven and earth by helping us to forgive. We sure have a lot of control over what we perceive!

49

April 29 — Defining the Time

Yesterday a host on one of the NPR radio shows said the upcoming discussion would seek to "define this moment in history." Would we look back on this as the time of "the economic collapse?"

We often review past times categorized by the bad things that happened. The emotional intensity engendered by facing difficulties can anchor our memories. Sometimes I catch myself categorizing memories asking if it happened before or after grandpa's death, 9/11, my diagnosis, or various other bad times. Yet I mostly anchor past events to the school I attended, which grade I was in or house I lived in, who were my best friends at that time, or what was my job.

As individuals or as a people we can choose how we define our time. Bad things do happen, but how we respond to those crises defines the time more than the crises themselves, revealing what is important to us: our values and motivations.

I remember a story my grandmother told of tramps knocking on her back door at dinner time during the great depression. Her family would welcome them in, and whatever food they had they shared. I remember being surprised that they weren't frightened by people wandering around their yard to come to the back yard. People defined that moment in history by their hospitality and lack of fear as much as or even more than by the financial hardship they faced. My grandmother's story showed the depression to be a generous time, at least for her and her family. I think we may be too afraid to be as hospitable and generous as we face the economic collapse of our own times. This picture shows the light penetrating through to the forest floor. My grandmother's story shed light on generosity and openness to strangers. What will our stories about our times reveal about us and these days decades from now?

May 6 — All Shall be Well

About 600 years ago in England Lady Julian of Norwich had a vision of the universe in the palm of God's hand. The whole universe simply looked like a hazelnut. She asked why it exists, and the answer came that God loved it into being and continues to sustain it in love.

In contrast to the simple image of a hazelnut, the complicated network of branches in the dogwood tree in my front yard suggests the universe to me today. And its beauty suggests it and the universe it is in has been loved into being and continues in that love.

As I pray for you and all who need healing today, I am reassured with the same words as Lady Julian was in her visions, "All shall be well, and all shall be well, and all manner of thing shall be well."

May 13 — Megaphones

This week the need for healing is great, so I am glad to have this azalea bush echo my prayers. Each flower looks like a megaphone boosting the volume. But just as the beautiful flowers echo my hope for your healing, I hear them echo God's message of reassurance and love. The beauty in creation is God's megaphone, too. It amplifies the reassurance of love expressed in God's Son.

Beauty in the world speaks to my spirit and tells me God is with us, speaking to us and listening to us, getting our attention and showing we have God's attention. This azalea is another burning bush. Through it God says here before me, "I am," and, "I hear you." What do you hear God saying through the beauty you can see around you? In what ways is it a sign God hears you?

May 27 — Lean Into Life

Usually my cards show photographs of nature, but for the first time I have chosen a people picture. I have been to all my kids' track meets to see them compete and to photograph the action. This picture of the start of the 800-meter dash captured my spiritual imagination. I love how the runners lean into the future. It seemed an apt metaphor for life—or at least for life when we start fresh.

I have always thought of "leaning on the everlasting arms" as a static leaning, like leaning against a post that doesn't move. The whole idea of leaning on the everlasting arms is much more appealing to me now that I think of it as leaning into new adventures with God. This strikes me as a rich source of fruitful metaphors:

hope: leaning into the future trusting God.

love: leaning into life with another person

prayer: leaning into God with possibilities to sort.

Is there ever a moment in life or death that God doesn't want us to lean into the change in store for us? Lean into any question to find a solution. How can you apply leaning in your life. Lean into life to find out….

June 9 —Flexibility

This past Sunday I read about Jesus saying, "The wind blows where it chooses, and you hear the sound of it, but you do not know where it comes from or where it goes" (John 3:8). If we are to understand him to mean the Holy Spirit by the wind, then it is surely true!

The issue is our control. We want to control it all, even God. That is our undoing. Twelve Step Programs like AA get it right when they make control the first issue to be dealt with in the first three steps. The challenge is to find that delicate balance where we can fly with the wind, but not be tossed to and fro by everything blowing by.

Perhaps we can learn from trees that face the wind with flexibility. They are not too rigid, so they are able to go with the wind, yet they are rigid enough to retain their identity. They move with the wind, but remain rooted.

Yes, I think we can learn a lot from how the wind blows through the trees: flexibility, balance, self understanding and confidence, to name just a few. What would you add to the list?

June 11 — Imagination

Even though I knew my colleague had been ill, I was shocked to hear he died today. I first thought, "Here he is sick himself, and his father must have died." Just for a moment my imagination kicked in to protect me and ease me into reality. A second later I realized it really was my friend, the man I saw just two days ago.

More thoughts came to mind: "I had just begun to pray for him." "I had just begun to send notes to him." I had imagined sending many homemade cards and brief reflections to him and his wife, but I started too late for him to get any. I had imagined..., but my imagination did not control reality.

I often think about imagination, as I have today, prompted by a concluding sentence for morning prayer, the one from Ephesians 3:20-21, "Glory to God whose power, working in us, can do infinitely more than we can ask or imagine: glory to him from generation to generation in the Church, and in Christ Jesus forever and ever." The concept of God being able to do more than I can imagine is very encouraging to me. After all, I can (and do) imagine a lot. Yet God can do more than that!

The words from Ephesians came to me again, when I looked at the picture I thought of as I prayed for my friend and his family, along with all the people on my list. It is a picture of a shadow. The reality I see—with injustice, hatred, sickness and death—is like a shadow compared to the reality I imagine. The reality I imagine is a shadow of what God can do. That bodes well for us all. It bodes well for my colleague who died.

In medieval times St. Anselm leveraged the concept of God (that than which nothing greater can be thought) into confident trust—even ontological proof of God's existence. At the dawn of modernity, Descartes leveraged thought into self-confidence, and self-confidence into confident trust in God (I think therefore I am… therefore God is). In these postmodern days, let us leverage our imagination into hope. In this hour of need, let us launch our imagination to soar high, trusting that it will ease us into the even greater reality of what God is up to—what God is doing.

Even now I imagine my late colleague, an ever practical thinker, commenting, "If imagination helps those who mourn, it's ok." And I imagine commenting back, "If God can do more than you or I can imagine, it's more than ok." Imagine it all—life and even death—better than we can imagine it. Go on! Now in this hour of need, we better not let our imagination languish. Imagine the best. Whatever you think that is, believe God is doing even better, and realize that what God does is so good it has to be.

June 20 — God's Brain: Left and Right

A memory is not the experience. A map is not the route on the ground. An architect's plan is not the building. We rely on simplifications of all sorts to help us take in reality in a useful way. Even our self-understanding is enriched by models that are less than who we are.

I had fun yesterday with one such oversimplification: the notion that our right brains control our creativity, our left brains control our orderliness, and one or the other side is dominant. After quickly figuring out which side is dominant in me (and giving you something to ponder) I had fun wondering about God's right and left-brain—or at least the characterization of the right and left-brains. I began by considering the first creation story in Genesis where God creates in very orderly fashion, by logical progression. The process is presented as a left-brain exercise.

How surprising! I don't think of left-brain processes as creative in themselves! If we look at the story more closely, tucked in so one could easily miss its importance, find the Spirit hovering over the deep. There is the Right Brain initiating the creative stance. Before this there was nothing. The Spirit hovers and there is a deep. The rest is, as they say, history. The Left Brain took charge, called creation forth, tidied things up by category, and evaluated it all, judging creation to be very good. Then God rested. Was the nap needed by the Right Brain? (I would need rest to stay creative.)

Jesus challenged the religious leaders that overemphasized the Left Brain of God—the legalistic settled, unchanging mind of God. Jesus called for a balance that gives due respect to the dynamic creative mind of God—the wind that blows where it wills unexpectedly and unpredictably. Anglicans try to follow his example in a dynamic creative way, which often puts us at odds with certain left-brain-dominant branches of the church!

The Gospel recently read in church drew a distinction between forgivable sin and unforgivable sin, blaspheming the Holy Spirit. Jesus doesn't explain what that distinction really is, but I think this Right/Left Brain oversimplification opens up a way to make sense of it. We might categorize forgivable sin as offenses against the orderliness of God, offending God's

Left Brain. But somehow we are undone by our denigration of the Right Brain of God.

Jesus promised he would send the Holy Spirit to lead us into all truth. I don't see this as a Left Brain exercise—a logical progression of categorizing and formulating knowledge. I see it as a right brain exercise—of stirring things up, looking at them in fresh ways, and developing wisdom.

Jesus promised to send the Comforter. Are we comforted by the unchanging orderliness of God—the Left Brain of God, or the God that loves us into being through creative forces that overwhelm even death—the Right Brain of God? I suppose I find both comforting when I need a rest, but when I want to restart—when I want new life, I find the unpredictable creative side of God most refreshing, and therefore most comforting. We can rest assured: both dimensions of God are available to comfort us however we need to be comforted—by orderliness or by creativity.

To say I love both the Right Brain and the Left Brain of God is true, but my love for the Left Brain of God is like intellectual appreciation. I love the Right Brain of God with passion that resonates with the creative impulse.

I really don't think God is or has a right brain or a left-brain, anymore than I think the map shows me the real route, or my memory captures the whole experience. Scripture refers to the heart of God, and the mind of God, but never the left or right brain of God. Nonetheless, this has been an insightful exploration of the mind of God, and fun, too.

July 14 — Open Minds

Though I have not sent a card for a few weeks, I have held you in prayer, ever confident that God's healing grace is not confined to my cards. My routine was disrupted when I was away for a week, and since I returned, I haven't felt well. I am tempted to describe the hiatus as it says in 1Samuel 3:1, "In those days the word of the LORD was rare; there were not many visions." But I wouldn't dare! That would undermine one of the sermons inside me—they say every preacher only really has four or five. You probably know by now one of mine is this: Expect God to always have a message for you packaged in reality. I can only say, the last few weeks my eyes and ears have not noticed many messages from God. I did see some sights that illustrated some of my "sermons inside". For example, I watched a woodpecker on an old log. The bird pecked like a lumberjack would use an axe: first from one side, then the other. I thought of how I challenge people to get at things from different angles. You may have heard me suggest that we get more out of life by looking at it from both scientific and religious perspectives.... At Morning Prayer last Thursday, these words from Luke 24:45 struck me: "Then he opened their minds so they could understand..." So that's the key to understanding: open minds! Again, this resonates with one of my main messages to the world: be open-minded! It's not a fresh challenge for me.

Or is it? Perhaps I should consider how I am closed-minded. That may lead me towards healing. You could help me: I invite you to pray for me to be open minded, particularly at two times in my life: "now and at the hour of my death". It is obvious why now, but why at death? For heaven's sake! Hell would be constructed by self-exiled close-minded people who reject heaven because it is not exactly like they pictured it from whatever book they hold dear. You know what I mean if you have ever gone to a movie with someone who can't enjoy it if it differs from the book.

59

Join me in praying that we always be open to God exceeding our expectations. We often don't realize that is what God is always up to. We miss it because our closed minds fail to understand reality, much less the various versions of it we find shared in a book or movie or even a greeting card. May God open our minds....

July 26 — Perfected Power

When I saw the first morning glory in my garden, I was very excited. I react to each new bloom as if I were a kid at Christmas, or, and this makes sense given the star pattern, like a wise traveler at Epiphany. I love it! I was struck by the blossom growing not on the healthy looking leafy plant on the right side of my driveway, but on the scraggly struggling plant on the left side.

Sometimes struggling and scraggy myself, I took pleasure in this. I thought of God's response to St. Paul's prayer, "My power is made perfect in weakness." May it be so with us. I also was amazed how the flower glowed with translucent beauty. The Creator's glory shone through it. While we are more opaque and dense, may it be so with us! May the morning glory inspire you and brighten your day, too.

61

August 3 — Perfect Imperfections

The globe thistle in my garden is a perfect globe of little flowers or florets, each one a star, unique and imperfect. Together they are beautiful—a wonderful image of community.

August 18 — Serene Scene

I share with you the peace God shared with me last week while camping in New Hampshire. Several mornings I took out the kayak at dawn to think, pray, and take pictures. May this serene scene evoke peace in you, too.

August 20 — Turbulent Presence

Last week while kayaking on the pond in New Hampshire, I tried to capture with my camera a star that floated on the pond's surface. It supported a three inch stem with a small yellow flower bud. It was so delicately balanced that each time I drew near enough to photograph it from my kayak, the turbulence of my presence toppled the tower.

It reminded me of Babble and humanity's aspirations to see the world from God's perspective—from outside the world. I thought of the uncertainty principle of Heisenberg which proves our presence in the world, and our impact on it, limits our ability to see it all. There is no surgery without the cutting of tissues, no war without collateral damage, no mining without disrupting the land, and no observing the world without affecting it. I cannot capture all beauty to share it. Some of it is spent or consumed in the experience of it. As my father says, "You cannot have your cake and eat it, too."

Or can you? Have I drawn you in to experience in your own mind the beauty of the delicate balance of the flower floating on a star? Is this message a sacrament that makes the beauty present still?

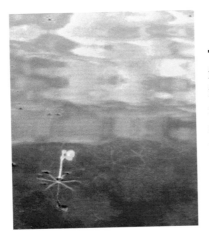

Three years later I photographed the same species of flower, a yellow floating bladderwort. It is named for its bladders which are arranged as in a star, on which it so delicately floats. This time I was in a canoe, which sits higher than a kayak, allowing a less turbulent perspective of the lake. Or did I glimpse space out there amongst the clouds?

August 21 — Multiple Perspectives

What was it about these plants and their reflection that fascinated me as I kayaked last week? I marveled at God's artistry. I think it was the multiple textures and perspectives presented to the eye all at once—the sharp angles and smooth curves, the view of both the top and bottom. As I thought about this, I wondered, "Is this a model for community?"

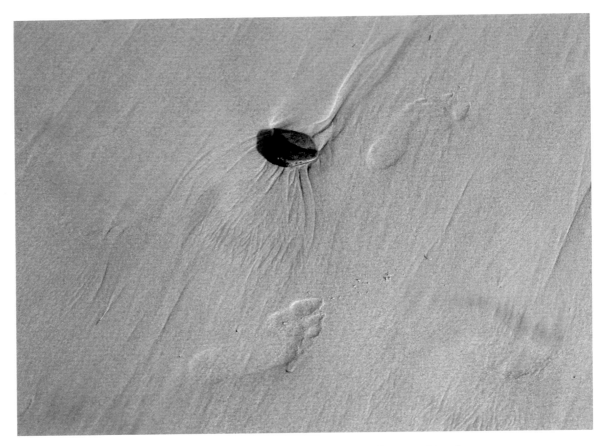

August 31 — The Truth About Beige

A friend once lied to me when I asked her favorite color. "Blue," she said. A couple of years later we laughed as she confessed she really liked beige. She had lied, afraid that I would think she were boring if she told the truth.

Color dazzles me. I love to look in my kitchen cabinet full of over twenty place settings, each a different color. My wardrobe includes lots of color, too, and color is my garden's specialty.

Yet this scene of sand, shaped by a walking woman and waves retreating around a rock, reveals the truth—beige is beautiful, and blessed be the eyes that see that beauty.

September 9 — An Image of Inspiration

This morning as I photographed a bumble bee on agastache, it was not the strange beauty of the flower that I wanted to capture, but rather how attractive the flowers were to the bees. They seem to love the agastache, and are driven with a passion for more.

When I dropped my daughter off at college this weekend, the dean spoke to the parents about the college's goal to help the students discover the subject that attracts them. It may be a strange subject the students have not yet been exposed to, but when they explore it they discover it inspires a passion that drives them towards their life's work.

The bee's attraction to the agastache is a symbol of this quest for the inspiration each of us must find to become a happy adult. I wonder: does the quest ever really end? Even though I found my life's work long ago, my quest continues. Sometimes I have refined and narrowed my focus; other times I have expanded it as I integrate more and more into it; and I have had to accommodate changes necessitated by life. I expect the process never ends, especially if we approach life seeking the best blossom around—the best steps to take next.

This flower and bee remind me to brighten each day with a beautiful discovery that has the power to drive me. Everywhere I look I can find something, and when my place in the world shrinks to where I cannot find it out there, I trust that God's perfect passion will continue to inspire me through the indelible image of all the beauty written by God's hand within my soul, the imprint of life's many inspirations discovered all along the way.

September 14 — To Capture, Package, and Share

These Black Eyed Susans captured the sunlight, packaged it as beautiful flowers, and shared it with me. Likewise, I captured hope for your health and wellbeing, packaged it as a prayer, and shared it with God. It occurs to me that all of it—both the flowers and my prayer—are packages shared with us by God who has captured a bit of divine love and grace, and shared it with us in a way that draws us up and into it all. It is this process that I seek to capture and package to share with you through these words and this picture.

September 21 — Surprise in Perfection

I took hundreds of photographs of this butterfly in a quest for the perfect shot. And some of those pictures approach what I might expect perfection would be. So why did this photo draw me in instead of the more perfect ones?

This picture packs surprises. At first glance it looks upside down, but the photo is right side up. The butterfly's wings, with their right angle and elegant curvature, invite me to follow. They reassure me by pointing the way beyond, onward and upward. The back end of an upside down butterfly reveals this secret of perfection—that its allure lies not in its conformity to expectations but rather in the surprises discovered among our expectations.

October 16 —The Forest Through the Trees

It is said, "You can't see the forest through the trees," but yesterday in my backyard I could! Though I was still in the shade, the early morning sun shone so I could see beyond my own little world. What I saw was glorious. The bright glory of the scene reminded me of The Absorbeat, a prayer of St. Francis in which he describes the love of God as "fiery and sweet as honey". How glorious it was to see this sign of the love of God, a love which inspires hope by reminding us to look beyond. I took a picture of that sign so I could share it with you and brighten your day, too.

The Absorbeat

a prayer of Saint Francis, amended

May the power of your love, Lord Christ,
fiery and sweet as honey,
wean my heart from all that is under heaven,
so that I may live and die for love of your love,
who were so good as to live and die
for love of my love. Amen.

November 1 – 30 – Poems for Literacy

During the thirty days of November 2009 I participated in a fundraising event, "30 Poems in 30 Days," organized by the Poet Laureate of Northampton to benefit the Family Literacy Project of the Center for New Americans. Some of those poems were shared with Laurel, and so they are included here.

Intimidating Leaves

The leaf pile looked huuuuge
It would take days to pick up!
No! Twenty minutes.

November 5

Oak Leaves on the Rail Trail

Leaves lie on my path,
Angles and curves of beauty,
And no two alike!

November 8

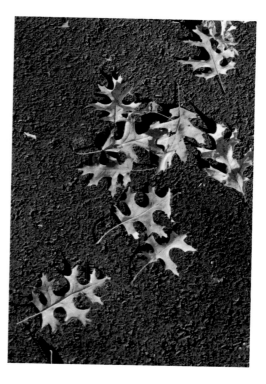

*Four Poems About Beautiful Music
Written November 13 and 14*

Beautiful music,
Fulfilled expectant surprise,
Wakens hope for life.

Resistant beauty—
Raucous rebellions of sound—
"Yes, I'm here to stay!"

Hear beauty still
Old souls soothed by melodies,
"Yes, I will go on."

Music sets us free:
Loud lifts up and launches us;
Soft lands us in peace.

November 19 — The One Word

God is willing to speak and listen
To whatever we've said or sung,
But when not stooping to our lowly position
What be God's native tongue?

God speaks a living language of love,
Its vocabulary is only one Word,
But without understanding the grammar above
Its translation is impossibly absurd.

As the English speak English, so God speaks God,
But the difference is profound,
For when God speaks God, what comes out is odd,
It's something other than sound.

When God speaks God, as God always does,
What emerges is God given up.

This makes room for all whom God loves,
God sacrificing God for us.

For when God speaks, God says "Me."
Which a liberator hears, "I AM."
In emptiness we hear, "Let there be…"
But evil hears only, "Damn!"

What is heard depends on inflection and voice,
But the vocabulary is always the same.
Which meaning's intended is not our choice,
One's relationship with God is to blame.

Imagine with wonder what happened one day
When the Word was expressed as a man.
What was God here trying to say?
It's still the self sacrificing plan.

Living in flesh death had to be faced.
Would that put an end to it all?
No, for God's Word has always embraced
The undoing of God's self for all.

So thank Jesus Christ—this message of love
Expressed in the language of God.
Hear the Lord give up "Me" from above.
"I am, too," answer, awed.

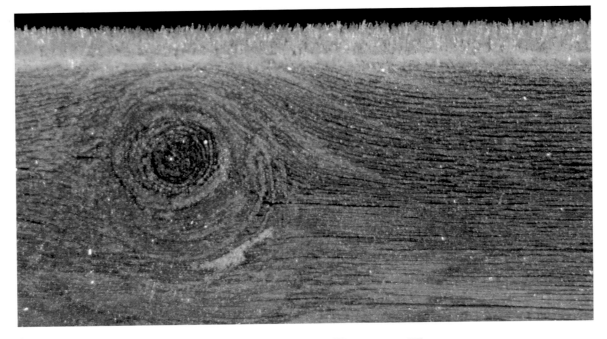

November 23 — Camera Eye

Give me a camera,
And the world is changed
By my looking for
The perfect framing,
A good angle,
Color, shadow, lighting,
And line,
All with an eye for beauty.

I don't even have to
Look through the camera.
Just holding it in my hands
The camera changes how I see.
It's amazing how
Seeking beauty
Changes everything.

November 26 — A Thanksgiving Haiku Feast

Store shelves always full--
So much good food to choose from,
Thanks to all involved.

Football on the field,
Then dinner at the table,
End with football from the couch.

Plenty on the plates,
People we love all around,
Thanksgiving dinner!

The wine in the glass,
A bounty set before us,
Cheers our thankful hearts.

We made it this far,
Now we face the cold winter,
Let's pause and give thanks.

What a strange custom:
Give thanks by eating too much,
Then shop the next day.

Wait, it's Thanksgiving!
We forgot to say a blessing!
Eat after we pray!

Thanksgiving pressures
Bad jokes, forced grace, belt too tight,
But think of the bird!

2010

"Good relationships bring us into the present and in that moment introduce us to forever, not as something to wait for, but something already changing us now."

July 2 — Reality is Relationship

February 2 — Inspired By Need

I have been waiting for fresh inspiration to share with you: an insight or two and a photograph of beauty I find around me, but none has caught my attention. Nonetheless, my prayers are full of hope for those of you who grieve, those who are sick, and those with other needs.

If we were hungry, we would not wait to eat fresh food with a cupboard full of stored food. Likewise, though I have no fresh wisdom to share or recent picture to send, I am motivated by my soul's resonance with your need and God's ever fresh desire to brighten your day. Stored in this photograph of a garden in Stanley Park is summer warmth and beauty that has neither gone stale or spoiled. May it encourage and delight you.

February 14 — Color the Darkness

I experimented with a photograph of the full moon from January. It was too dark, much as some news from friends this past month has been too dark for me. When I applied variations of light and color to the picture, and put those variations together, the result was beautiful. It reminded me of what we hope for when we pray—that God bring light and color to the darkness we face and put the pieces of our lives back together in a beautiful way. That is my prayer for you.

February 21 — Threshold Adjustments

After a recent snow storm fizzled on its way north to us, my son asked if there was enough snow to cross country ski. I told him there wasn't. Yet I wonder if my snow sufficiency threshold was set too high! How appropriate to think about that threshold as the sunny days reduce the likelihood of enough snow falling. Still I have hope as a snow storm is in the forecast for mid-week.

I started thinking about thresholds in church today. They came to mind as I remembered in December the snow was so beautiful as it melted away. If only I had lowered my snow sufficiency threshold back in Advent, we could have skied early this winter! Oh well. Late is a good time to ski, too.

Would adjusting thresholds be a good spiritual discipline for Lent? After church a chaplain spoke about people waiting to forgive until the end is near. Though he described his role in different terms, he helps them lower their forgiveness threshold so the end is more peaceful. I thought why wait to do it so I can die at peace; forgive so I can live at peace for a long time!

This Lent I can think of many more thresholds to consider and adjust. Why wait to clean until an hour before guests arrive? I notice, too, that some of us speak most harshly to the people we love the most. There's a threshold many should raise! By Easter, I'll clean house, forgive as though a good life depended on it, and tell my loved ones of my love. Oh! And I'll take my son cross country skiing the first chance we get!

March 2 —
A Hopeful
Breakthrough:
Variations
on a Theme

Yesterday God got my attention with the beauty hidden in an ugly hole in the snow. In that hole daffodils were breaking through. I saw it as a hopeful sign: "Flowers are on the way! There is much more to come!" But how could I highlight the beauty? I tried by playing with the color. I share some results with you. Which if any of the variations inspire you to be hopeful, or brings you joy, or sends you

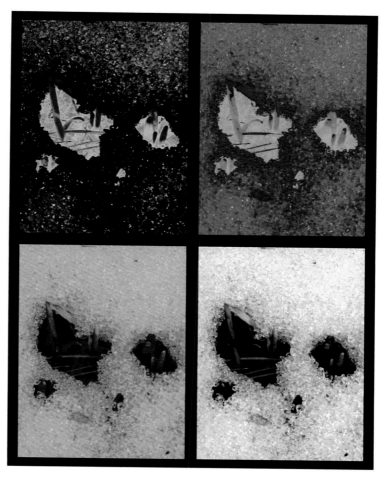

towards your own breakthrough? Which captures best the movement towards Easter? I like the brown version—the first in the series above. It suggests to me the perspective of the bulb underground, inspired by its hopeful dreamlike vision of a world beyond its view, a world where the daffodil belongs, a world that will be all the more beautiful for having the daffodil in it.

Yet even more than that, in the end, after dreams and visions, I like the picture that shows reality. All we do to change our view is truly good only if it helps us see more clearly what really is before our very eyes.

March 12 — Waking Up After Winter

Some early signs of spring surprised me in my garden today. I was most surprised by the Pulmonaria, or lungwort. I found it peeking out from under the winter blanket of leaves and needles. I didn't expect to see it flowering so soon, about three weeks earlier than last year. Pink when they first emerge, Pulmonaria flowers become blue or lavender, as they mature. The plant is bright, suggesting bold confidence in its contribution of its fresh but mature perspective. The plant remains open to the world with no sense of shame for being different than it once was, no swooning for past glories.

The brightly colored lilac buds also drew my attention with their bundles of beauty about to burst. They sparked my imagination. Do you think the lilac buds look like a bishop's mitre? The red ones look like a bishop praying at the altar.

I hope these signs of early spring spark your imagination and bring you a bit of joy. I hope they get you to think about your own aging process. May these signs brighten your day in a way that encourages you to brighten your world with your own unique beauty.

March 19 — Without Words: Morning Prayer (below) /
Afternoon Praise (above)

April 2 — Light Transforming the Dark

Early in the morning yesterday, Good Friday, I looked out my back window, and quickly went for my camera. I wanted to capture and share the scene. The strange view was rosy and bright above and blue and still dark below. One friend saw the picture posted on Facebook and commented, "Both eerie and beautiful at the same time..." I thought it suggested the theology of the day: light transforming the dark.

A preaching professor once told me, "There has to be a lot of Easter in a Good Friday sermon, and a lot of Good Friday in an Easter sermon. The same is true of a good photograph relative to light and darkness. The goal is to bring light to the darkness. Its aim is hope.

I send this on the day in between Good Friday and Easter, wishing you the best yesterday, today, and tomorrow. May light always shine to bring beauty to you and your struggles in the fog or in the dark.

June 24 — Gold From Deep Within

The allium bulbs I planted last fall broke ground this spring, and produced beautiful globes in early June. Now in late June, they are golden. All along the way they have been beautiful, at least to me. Partly that is because I have chosen to see the beauty of the moment, but it also is because these alliums show me beauty in the context of change.

It wasn't until the moment I put the two images side by side, that I saw the beauty of the younger blossoms lies mostly on the surfaces. This was especially evident side by side, for in this context I saw how the beautiful surface of the fresh blossoms is a wall hiding what lies within. The depths can be glimpsed, but are well defended behind the beautiful surface.

The aged blossoms have dropped their defenses. I can see beauty emanating from deep within each globe. They invite us to mine their golden treasure.

July 2 — Reality is Relationship

While waiting for my son at a park, I walked around taking pictures of the beautiful gardens. These flowers caught my eye because of the way they relate to each other. They look like lovers, alive and luminescent. They suggest to me the nature of reality: that it is relationship.

While waiting for the dentist today I read a Scientific American article, "Is Time an Illusion" in the June 2010 issue. The author, Craig Callender, explains that time is not needed to describe the changing universe. Time emerges in the context of the changing relationships. So we even must abandon the notion that reality is the relationship between things more or less moving through time. No! Reality, even time, and even the things that are real—all matter—all that matters, are all dynamic relationships. Reality is relationship.

Even as I write this, part of me says, "No, wait! Reality is things, and ultimately it is perfect, ideal, un-relating things." But think about what is most important. Is it ultimately static things? I would say not. What is most important is change in a relationship—how it grows, deepens, and develops—how it shapes time and me. Yes, our relationships with God and others shape even eternity. Good relationships bring us into the present and in that moment introduce us to forever, not as something to wait for, but something already changing us now. This is what beauty is all about: bringing me into the present and into eternity, both at the same time, or rather both beyond time!

July 4 & 27— Stars and Swirling Stripes
Garden Symmetry Series

July 16 — Big Ben and Westminster Abbey
(as seen from the Eye of London)

This photograph, taken while visiting relatives in England, shows two great buildings side by side: Big Ben towers over the halls of politics while next door the steeples of Westminster Abbey tower over the church. This picture suggests the institutions stand side by side in competition. The buildings make me wonder which will have the louder voice. Which will define the times? Does faith inform politics? Is it any different in the United States, where we strive for a clear separation between the two?

I get a whole different feeling if I switch the basic question around: does politics inform faith? The question makes me cringe! It is hard to acknowledge that faith should be informed by anything so temporal. Politics encompasses the realm of compromise. Faith must stand uncompromising. Or so we think.

Compromise involves the humble acknowledgment that one does not hold all the power, and to move forward one must accept some input from other people who also have power. At its best in both politics and faith, power is grounded in values, such as the value of an individual in contrast to the value of a group. The more narrow the range of values, the more narrow the politics and faith. If I can broaden the range to recognize some value in others' positions, then I can compromise without losing my integrity. In the end it all may come down to deciding in order to keep the relationship.

Imagine yourself on judgment day, standing before God, who tells you that you got everything right about faith except the pronunciation of the name of Jesus. Surely you would agree to change such a trivial detail to keep the relationship. Hopefully that would be true no matter how precious the name's mispronunciation had become.

What if God challenged you for not living into the full stature of the image of God—for not being creative, or for exercising your dominion in an abusive way? Would you accept forgiveness and move on, or get held up by an uncompromising faith?

Compromising faith is forgiving faith. We forgive and are forgiven by the compromise of justice and mercy. Forgiveness facilitates a good relationship with God and each other. That is what Jesus offers, reconciled relationships through forgiveness.

The Bible quickens in me values that inform my decisions. Problems arise when I make choices based on fewer passages and fewer values. For example, if I were to read the Bible in a more superficial and narrow manner, then passages that mention slaves might suggest that God approves of slavery. I might accept that point of view because I know God loves me as someone special and God wants me to prosper. Yet I reject slavery because I see as far more important the sovereign value of each image of God and the call to love others no less than I love myself.

I mention slavery because it is generally acknowledged to be a clear rejection of the will of God and the bulk of God's values. It is humbling to realize that in our nation and the church many of our forbearers clung to the wrong position because they held an uncompromising faith. Indeed, it is a great irony that the integrity of our faith—its ability to establish and maintain a close relationship with God—is easily compromised if we do not hold a compromising faith.

Today our society is in turmoil as our view of homosexuality shifts. Some still choose to emphasize those verses of Scripture that condemn homosexuality, but more and more of us choose to heed the call to love and not judge. We could presume to hold the power to change a person into a bundle of sticks to be burned. Instead we wield the power to change a bundle of sticks into a person. Why would any of us cling to an uncompromising faith and the compromised relationship with God and others when it becomes clear how that faith twists reality and leads to death?

Compromising faith is living. It allows for growth and change. It welcomes the Holy Spirit who will lead us into all truth, revealing the will of God by ever clarifying God's values and instilling them in us. Compromise in politics is no less important.

July 19 — On the Back of a Motorcycle
My Third Cousin Gives My Son a Ride

My son and I went on a father-son trip to England and Iceland. It was a wonderful adventure—eye opening in some ways. We did a few tourist things, like ride the Eye of London (a large Ferris wheel), we went to Stonehenge, and we ate at the Hard Rock Café. A highlight was the Beetles tour of London, ending at Abbey Road Studio, where I photographed my son walking across Abbey Road in the position of John Lennon on the Abbey Road album.

These were all wonderful activities, but the most memorable experiences for me were watching my son relate to the English people: He went trail biking with some middle aged adults. He borrowed his fourth cousin's bike and put up with rust and bad brakes to keep up with the very fit older men. My son played soccer (or as they say, football) with a men's team during one of their practice scrimmages. He has not played for a couple of years, and the young men were generally better than he, but he did not embarrass himself. He played guitar for two hours and fifteen minutes in an English pub with a pick up band. Within five minutes the other musicians made him lead guitar. He was impressive, surprising us how entertaining he could be. And he jammed with another fourth cousin, an excellent guitar player, but not so good at playing with others. Yet my son humbly played along with him. Witnessing these experiences was wonderful!

August 10 — Hopeful Lines of Light

a haiku inspired by this picture,
photographed and written while praying
for healing for some friends in need.

Fog lit by sunshine,
Beaming through gaps in the trees:
Hopeful lines of light.

Last night's rain lingers,
Clinging to a budding branch,
To welcome the day.

How I Pray for You
When I pray for you
In my mind I bring you before God,
To the place where "I am"
And you can be, too.

It is best to be there in the moment,
At least for me because I forget.
I need no access to memory.
To bring hope into the present.

So when I pray for you,
Prayer is not saying names before God.
I may not remember your name there,
I know names elsewhere if at all.

When I pray for you
I bring you as you are, sick,
And as I am, broken,
Reality in the presence of God.

(continued next page.)

My prayer is not dimmed
By the pattern and color of our health
Clashing with divine well being,
Though the clash be so great.

We would be undone by the difference,
Were not the deeper beauty within us
Illuminated by light with proven power
To pierce the darkness of death.

Neither is my prayer silenced
By the deafening dissonance
Between the sound of sickness
And the harmonies of heavenly health.

As I speak and listen before God,
I tune in to divine well being,
Seeking our mystical resonance
With the glorious songs sung there.

This I do not know;
I feel this—I see and hear it.
When I pray for you,
Do you feel it, too?

August 30 — Free to Be Wrong

For months I have thought about the importance of the freedom to be wrong. The issue was raised by a column posted by a friend on Facebook, and then I was spurred on by baseball. Remember the imperfect call which made a perfect baseball game imperfect? Umpire Jim Joyce called Jason Donald safe at first, in what should have been the last out of Armando Galarraga's perfect game. Baseball knowingly builds into its structure imperfect judgment for the sake of the flow of the game. Even when it later is shown to be wrong, the swift judgment stands. The rules of the game move the action along by freeing the umpire to be decisive, whether right or wrong.

In real life we can be more patient with many decisions, allowing input from sources, both human and technological. Yet sooner or later we have to risk being wrong and decide. If we later find we made a wrong decision we often can change our minds, but not always. A wrong decision may cost us dearly. But to delude ourselves that we are always right could cost us much more: a civil society.

I propose this simple test to help us determine if we mistakenly reject the possibility that we are wrong. Ask yourself three questions:

1. What do we defend? If we are free to be wrong, then we are free to defend the powerless. If we are not free to be wrong then we will soon be defending ourselves, the institutions we represent, the gods we believe in, or our notion of truth—nearly anything other than the defenseless.

2. Do we listen to others? If we cannot be wrong, we will not listen to others. We will shut our ears and our minds, but probably not our mouths. We will speak to tell our point of view, not to talk with others or to discuss. We will isolate ourselves as our language is marked by vitriol, anger, and fear and we alienate those who disagree. We will think it good and righteous and patriotic that we live in a polarized society struggling in a culture war. Of course we will honestly believe that we are the faithful and trustworthy remnant. We will build walls on our borders to keep outsiders out. We will miss the irony that this most visible wall is not nearly as effective as the unseen walls we build to protect us from the ever growing "them". We will construct these walls because we will demonize our enemies. After all, who would listen to an enemy?

3. Do we resist change? Our resistance to say we are wrong will always lean us toward an unhealthy conservatism. We will ignore how the way things are is increasingly becoming a problem. We will condemn those who grow uncomfortable or object, convincing ourselves that they are the problem.

How did you do on this test? Are you free to be wrong? Or does my asking these questions make you want to defend God or America or your approach to reality? Please be concerned if you jump to the conclusion that I am the problem for raising these questions. I mean, really now, why would a few questions make you think of me as an enemy? If you wish to silence me, won't that prove that I am right?

September 5
Magnification

While visiting family in Maine, I noticed their mint variety attracted interesting insects. What a perfect opportunity to practice using my new telephoto lens.

The experience made me think of Saint Mary because of how she summed up what she was doing: "My soul magnifies the Lord." This is my mission, too, although I would add, *"and the world."*

I magnify the Lord and the world through my photography, zooming in on the Great Artist's art to find a meaningful message.

I also magnify the world through prayer, setting before God you—your need and hopes.

I don't pray to get God's attention or to get God going; You come up in my prayers because you already have God's attention—God is already working in you—and I am invited to be part of the whole process.

With all this magnification, does anything actually expand? What is shown remains the same size, but those who see, grow. Minds expand as they open more and more. Hearts expand to hold more and more love. Wills expand with stockpiles of resolve. All this magnification brings us to join God in what God is doing.

September 29 — Be Patient!

I had given up the expectation that this morning glory would ever flower. I planted it indoors around Saint Patrick's Day, but once I transplanted it, the vine grew very slowly. The rain yesterday seems to have given it what it needed to finally flower. High above my head, just above the trellis on my deck, the blue flower against the blue sky reminded me of thin and delicate wings.

This is the day the church celebrates the feast of Saint Michael the Archangel, and all angels. Their wings are symbols of their speed, which is why it is funny that the wings made of the morning glory petals convey a slower message: "Be patient and don't abandon hope". Add the usual angelic encouragement: "Fear not!" and we receive a worthy message from this beautiful flower.

October 7 — Larger Life

"Life is good," the t-shirts tell us. My daughter has one that shows a horse. My son's has a young person playing a guitar. My wife has one that shows someone relaxing by a campfire. There are many many images of the good life.

When I celebrate the Eucharist in a context where the chalice and paten are first covered by the veil, after communion I am deliberate as I put the veil back over the now empty vessels. I do this to remind us that the goodness we experience in life gives us merely a glimpse. This action hints of a promise: at some point the veil will be removed forever.

One of my favorite images from the Psalms is offered to help us understand how God is our refuge. One might expect the Psalm to thank God for protection, but God is praised for giving us "a drink from the river of your delights" (Psalm 35:8). A mere sip changes how we look at everything, and so, the praise continues, "In your light we see light" (Psalm 35:9).

Joy is how we see things after the sip. This joy permeates our perspective, and allows us to face anything. One little sip of God's love changes everything because it opens our hearts to receive and trust in the power of love.

Life is a glimpse, a sip, and….a third little image for the good life that I think of today: a deposit. God offers us the Holy Spirit as a deposit, a down payment, or a guarantee (2 Corinthians 5:5). As we enjoy the experience of

98

the Holy Spirit—as we are comforted, challenged, and delighted—God invites us to understand this experience as a promise there is much more to come. Anyone whose heart has welcomed the Holy Spirit understands this. We have experienced a partnership that points towards a deeper, more powerful intimacy with God.

The beautiful tree in this photograph helps me glimpse more.

- This picture delights me as it lifts the veil; it brings me before God where the tree of life is found, from which God gives me a sip.

- As I look at this picture, I open my heart to welcome any breeze from God, even the faintest breath rustling the leaves.

- The interplay of light allows my eye to better see light. These leaves brighten our day, sharing the light even during these darkening days when soon, we know, the leaves will fall. They are a sign of what St. Paul says we all want: mortality being swallowed up by life (2Corinthians 5:4).

It is easy to see how life is made small—too small—by even our long distant and eventual death. Thank God we know that what is small can be a sign of what is big. We may live this life made large by little experiences of larger life. I pray that our experience of the temporary prepare us for the permanent, our experience of the small, shape us for the big, our experience of reality tune us into what is really real.

99

November 2 — Usher Us Up

I love how these trees usher us upwards beyond their reach. They present their case in a beautiful way, and invite those who look up, "You take it from here now." Gazing up from beneath the trees, I knew I stood upon the ground in which they were rooted, yet the trees drew me onward and upward. They invited me to fly.

This experience reminded me of an idealistic friend who died in October, Emmett, one of the people to whom I send these messages. He was a peace activist, an advocate for the poor, a poet, and a priest. His ministry on the

streets was rooted in idealism and faith. He invited us to fly with similar ideals and faith. He has led as far as he could, ushering us upward beyond his reach. In life he invited all to join him in bearing witness. In death he invites us to take it from here...

As I think of Emmett, you, and me, I realize we all in some measure are like these trees, limited in our reach, but inviting others to go beyond our limits. We usher them upward, inviting them to fly. This is the challenge in parenting, ministry, teaching, and all the various expressions of love.

December 3 — Two Views of Nothing

Something different for Advent: Two poems about nothing, written to keep everything in perspective—to see reality as something.

Nothing

Picture nothing,
Then something.
That emerges
By chance?
Sucked into being by the lack?
However it happened,
All's still nothing—
On balance nothing—
And in the end nothing:
Enlightenment
To those who see.

Through Nothing

Picture God as all there is,
Nothing but!
But now notice—
Nothing but burgeoning emptiness,
In the hush hugged by hovering,
The pregnant pause before "Let there be…"

Suddenly the silence fills
With nothing but notes in nothing—
The song an irresistible invitation
Sung in welcome words so welcoming
To nothing but notes in nothing,
That everything nonetheless is.

We be echoes in the emptiness
Reverberations of resonance among rests,
For our score grants us voice—
To harmonize with heaven
And reach out through nothing,
Bridging the space in between.

Yet gaps widen and nothing grows
In the sound of "Let what be be for me."
NO!!! All is for nothing,
Unless it's through nothing—
Through that song of self sacrifice,
We reach out to sing, "Let there be…"

Hold onto nothing
And the world will be,
For we will let it be,
And the world will be very good.
As it be in the beginning,
Is now and forever be.

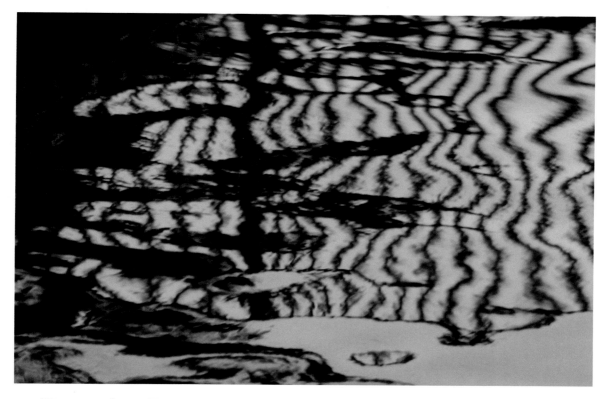

December 7 — From Negativity to Positive Thoughts

A friend of mine who is having surgery today was disturbed by people's comments about it being a bad day for surgery because bad things happened on Pearl Harbor Day. I share with you my encouragement to change the negativity into positive thoughts.

Pearl Harbor day is associated in my mind with Roger, a survivor of the attack on Pearl Harbor. He was a little man of great stature in my eyes. I knew him when he moved to Westfield and started coming to church. He passed away a few weeks ago, but he helped me see December 7th as a day of survival. He and others helped me see the day as a day that spurred great courage.

I think of Al who after the attack on Pearl Harbor lied about his age to enlist in the navy. He still is an inspiration, and I think he must be part cat—he survives many illnesses. He also is very well read! The day is a day that symbolizes our getting involved in the world, stopping our procrastination, taking action when action is called for.

December 7th is the day we remember Saint Ambrose. In the fourth century he was a peacemaker who went to a meeting where people were fighting about who should be bishop. After he exhorted them, both factions proclaimed, "Ambrose shall be our bishop." He had not even been baptized, but soon he was baptized and ordained deacon, priest, then bishop. So it is a day for wise choices, a day of peace, and a day of anointing. This is something Ambrose wrote:

103

Lord Jesus Christ, you are for me medicine when I am sick; you are my strength when I need help; you are life itself when I fear death; you are the way when I long for heaven; you are light when all is dark; you are my food when I need nourishment.

Ambrose baptized Saint Augustine so we are reminded we have blessings to bestow upon others. Whom will you bless in some way today? What story can you tell about how you have survived challenges, been motivated, or were selected for a role or task?

2011

"True love means God lives in the sod."

February 19 — In The Midst of the Mess

January 17 — Beautiful Path

Was the squirrel that made this path coming from the tree or going to it? An expert may be able to figure it out, but I can't.

Sometimes that is how life feels—like I don't know whether I am coming or going. Am I headed towards something or leaving something behind? I don't always know. When I grieve, it feels like I am leaving something or someone. In contrast, courtship or romance involves looking forward. But what about day-to-day life? Often life is so hectic, we are pulled in all directions at once! But I do know this: Just as the light brought out the beauty in the squirrel's path, the light can bring out the beauty on my path. I just need to keep my eyes open to see.

February 8 — Persistent Beauty

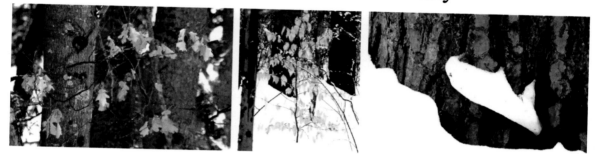

February 9 — Light Wisdom

This weekend a friend told me his wife was diagnosed with stage four ovarian cancer. I responded with love, stories of hope, and this reminder: "cancer is a word, not a sentence". The next day I tried to write a note for a new card, thinking I would start including this couple among the recipients. I set out to sum up all the wisdom from the more than 80 cards, including best phrases from past notes. The result was like a jackhammer of intensity! I was going about it all wrong. Overwhelmed, I went out with my camera as a way of praying for all of you, but soon settled as I focused on this leaf. What a contrast to my intense draft!

This leaf suggests a lighter message as it sits gently on top of it all. Neither the many feet of snow, nor any amount of heavy wintery mix has crushed it. Yes, the leaf has fallen—gravity always wins—but this leaf has done so with grace. It has endured well beyond expectations, having weathered many intense storms. I love how it points up in the general direction from whence it came. Could it also be expressing hope about ultimate plans?

The leaf reminds us wisdom is not weighty but light, not something to drag along from the past, but something that frees us to be well oriented in the present. I love how the leaf presents this wisdom to us in such a light and fresh way. Now, if only we could do as well!

February 19 — In The Midst of the Mess

Last night the wind brought back the cold, but not without using the snow as a canvas for a work of art. There is another way to look at it; I could also have said, "...not without making a mess."

What about us? Some people look at life as a mess; some people look at life as a work of art. Generally I encourage seeing the beauty, and today is no different, except there is a beauty you cannot see without seeing and acknowledging the mess. That is the beauty of God willing to meet us in the mess.

Meeting us in the mess — that's a way of summing up two Bible stories. To make the first human, God picked up dirt, molded it, and blew life inside. Taking that dirt is the first real contact between us and God. Eventually God united with the dirt by becoming one of us in Jesus.

To clean up the whole process and make it too immaculate is to deny the love that motivated the condescension, and worse: to deny the depth of God's union with us. So, yes I see the mess. And in the mess I find beauty. And the beauty changes how I see the mess: I will get through it with God.

My latest poems are about God joining us in the mess. I share two with you. I hope they brighten your day and any mess in your life.

Look Through the Dark

Thus says the Lord,
"Sure; you're a dirt balloon filled with my used air.
You are dust returning to dust;
But now welcome me if you dare,
I'll give you sight that sees by trust.

"This is the vision of the blessed:
They await my *inhaling* breath!
Look past the worst to the best;
See beyond darkness and death.

"They've heard the warning of prophets and sages,
'As dirt, keep a distance from God.'
But they opened the gift wrapped in darkness for ages,
'True love means God lives in the sod.'

"To look towards the future with hope,
Learn from mistakes of the past.
Nothing is helped by a grovel or grope;
Stand forgiven in God's love that'll last.

Since God took on the substance of stars—
The very stuff we're made of,
Take courage as God bears your pain and your scars,
See through the dark in light of love.

The Gospel According to Jesus the Incarnate

I am the messy conception,
I survived a scandalous debut,
Dirt for true incarnation,
For immaculate won't help God be you.

My mom? She wasn't perfect,
Practicing nagging as an art,
She'd search me for any defect,
And hold on to things in her heart.

My parents put on the pressure
With every story they'd tell,
And if about life I was unsure?
My God, it felt like hell!

My friends mostly were all jerks,
Misunderstanding whatever I'd say.
They showed me just how betrayal hurts.
Yes, for their sins I'd pay!

So trust me, I know life ain't easy.
Like you, I've faced the worst,
From anger or feeling sleazy,
To having such desire I'd burst.

Oh, I'm the messy incarnation,
Who survived a scandalous end,
Became dirt for true intervention,
Transfiguring stranger and friend.

April 21 — Hope for More

The lungwort in my garden is very beautiful this time of year with its flowers that start pink and turn light blue. This flower reminds me of my grandmother, perhaps because those colors were her favorite. Thinking of her, I am reminded of two stories that I hope would encourage anyone grieving.

The first is a story she told. My grandfather's grandmother was bedridden and unable to talk for the last seven years of her life. As my great great grandmother's death approached, her six living adult children gathered around her bed. Suddenly she sat up, looked at the door, and said, "Why Edward!" Then she fell back and died. Edward was a son that had predeceased her.

My grandmother told this story as evidence for the afterlife. She believed in more to come. When she told me that story, she had outlived two husbands whom she loved very much. She believed God would give her more blessings. It would be different, but it would be real and it would be more.

The second story reinforces the first. As my grandmother lay on her deathbed, my parents and siblings and I went to visit her, pray with her, and sing some hymns with her. It was around Thanksgiving. Of course, we sang the traditional "We gather together, to ask the Lord's blessing."

Her response to our singing at first confused us; she didn't exactly recognize us. She thought we might be angels. We knew she was no longer able to open her eyes, but confusing us with angels, well...perhaps her hearing was going, too!

My dad, who goes by "Dick", said, "It's Dick and his family here." She said, "Dick who?" Ouch!

It took some more conversation to determine that she wasn't confused. She just didn't know whether she was alive or dead. Was it her son, Dick, and his family, or her late husband, Dick, and an entourage of angels with family who had already died? My grandmother not knowing impressed upon me the depth of her confidence in God and eternity.

Because my grandmother trusted in God, she had hope. We believed Jesus' death, resurrection, and heavenly family reunion, makes our hope possible. (Hope was her middle name.)

I hope that every pink or blue flower any of us see, reminds us of our hope that through the love of God there is more....

May 10 — Color From Dirt

These flowers (Veronica peduncularis and Phlox subulata) inspired this haiku for the Easter season.

Color coaxed from dirt
Urges something from me:
Joy from emptiness.

2012

"I stand open because I stand secure in the embrace of a love so sure I need no other defense, no other assurance."

June 24 — Fear Not! Be Open!

January 21 — Persistent Gratitude

Oh leaf,
You scurried across
My snow covered yard,
Too fast to photograph
Until suddenly you stopped,
Stuck in the snow.
I wondered why you paused:
To strike a pose?
Or to check me out
As an animal in the zoo?
Did you slow
To smell me as a rose?
Was it for love?

I love how beautiful
You were on the snow:
Beauty I caught on camera,
Before heading in.
At the door I glanced back
And saw you had moved on
Without my thanks.

I understand
The way the world works—
It just happened:
You got stuck
For a brief moment.
It wasn't for you.
It wasn't for me.
I thank science for
Making gratitude irrelevant.

Oh leaf,
Since you didn't pause
To smell the roses,
To love or look for love,
I figure you stopped,
And I took your picture,
To cheer my friend.
In the end I thank her
For this glimpse
Of your beauty.

March 14 — The Mighty Conversation

As an expression of hope, I pray for you and keep on praying, because I know such love and concern shared with God can be mighty indeed. But if God were to send signs of love our way, wouldn't that be mighty, too? Yes! And that is exactly what I see in beauty: God talking to us. Beauty is all part of the conversation of prayer. It's the part we see or hear when we watch and listen.

Thank God there is humor in

the conversation, too. Consider the fluffy slipper…I mean, the weeping pussy willow's blossom. Weeping? Maybe weeping tears from laughter! I see serious beauty in how it can make us laugh. And one of the most beautiful things about all this beauty is that we can share it.

I share these glimpses of beauty I found today, hoping to brighten your day and I encourage you with the news that such beauty graces the mighty conversation with God held on your behalf.

May 14 — Painted Reality

While listening to the symphony orchestra play live, sometimes I take my glasses off and look at the stage. The musicians and their musical instruments suddenly look like an impressionist's painting (except it moves and makes music!). The distortions introduced by my natural vision are like a filter that makes reality impressionistic. In some funny ironic way this gives me the impression that I am able to add to the creative moment—all by blurring reality as if I were painting it.

Yet sometimes the more clearly I see reality, the more clearly I get the impression that reality already really is painted. My dogwood tree in my front yard gives me that impression every spring. Each petal looks as if it were a smudge of paint smeared by a brush which has left lines as a sure sign of the Painter's brushstroke. I am sure there is a scientific explanation—that the appearance serves to attract pollinators or to distract or deter potential threats. But just as an artwork may convey multiple meanings on different levels, could not reality do likewise?

I think the Painter intends for us to find additional meanings in the dogwood's beautiful design. Those lines point beyond survival to a richer life—a life enriched by creative expression. Though the design may be shaped and colored by practical and very important purposes (such as the

119

dogwood's survival), the design inspires joy and peace by conveying the world as art, especially good art that reveals something about the artist.

Because I get the sense that it is painted, and that the better I see, the more clearly that sense is conveyed, tells me that not all beauty is in the eye of the beholder. It is not all wishful thinking or mere projection. Reality really is beautiful. This incredible creativity of God does not condemn our blurring of reality, but we best not let our blurring blind us for long.

After our blurring of reality has done its work—after our rose colored glasses have filtered out the bad so we can learn to focus on the good, after denial has eased us towards the truth—the beauty out there invites us to face reality. We may see some ugliness, but I take courage in the fact the Painter clearly has painted beauty into it, too. Yes, each year the petals of my dogwood tree gently encourage me to see reality. Yes, there is beauty out there. But the reason I find this beauty so promising, is that each petal is painted fresh. This is no invitation back to a beginning. This beauty invites a fresh start.

June 21 — Living Life Well

This wasp surprised me. It looks strange with its long tail, striped body, and wing markings. When I first saw the wasp, I guessed that each trait served a defensive purpose. I looked with trepidation at the long stinger and speculated that the tail would break off if caught by a predator. I wondered if the wing spots were to mimic the eyes of a much larger creature. (I see a cat face complete with eyes, nose, and whiskers!) After all this speculation, I went in to check out wasps on the internet. I learned this wasp is in the family Ichneumonidae. The long stinger in some species can sting, but it is also an ovipositer. When the wasp senses the vibration of a larvae eating wood, that tail can drill in deep and deposit the wasp's fertilized eggs into the larvae. The tail is actually metal tipped as are the teeth of the wasp's larvae which can chew their way out of the depths. Do you see why this wasp amazed me?

Every characteristic is so well suited for its purpose, allowing the wasp to live well. What about us? Are we well equipped to live well? In all situations? That last bit of question brings me to think beyond physical limitations of the body (which already has given glimpses of its ultimate failure), and of things, for we all know, "You can't take it with you."

We do have one resource that enables us to live well in *all* situations: our human spirit. Think about it! Is there any situation that can stop the determined spirit from doing what the spirit does? The spirit can always love. We can always relate, strive to know and understand, experience life and live it. We can always seek beauty. We can always wonder, expressing our wonder in awe of the mystery, in worship, or in questions that lead us to discover more. We can always grow and learn. These endeavors of the spirit shape what it means for us to live well. They all require us to be open. There may be dangers to openness, but we cannot escape the fact that ultimately it is all that God demands of us. It is the first step of the spiritual life, and if there were a last step, it would be characterized by openness. Along the way, every step of progress involves openness. It is the essential attitude because it is required for a real relationship, and the spiritual life is nothing if not a relationship.

June 24 — Fear Not! Be Open!

Flowers fulfill their destiny by opening up. So do we, if our destiny is to live well no matter what. Unfortunately we can close our hearts and minds. We can shut down love; break off relationships, stop welcoming people, ideas, and change; cease learning, wondering, and questioning; and fail to live well. Why would we want that?

Fear, greed, guilt, addiction to power—these and other attitudes shut us down. We close our eyes to all but friend or foe. We listen for threats or praise. We become insecure, defensive, and longing for reassurance.

Faith, hope, love, trust, forgiveness—all these encourage us to open up and let go. (At least my faith does.) Angels tell us, "Fear not!" Prophets and teachers admonish us to give, to be humble, to liberate and empower, and to seek and offer forgiveness. Jesus set the most open, least defensive example. Indeed openness is encouraged, but what grace makes it happen?

I stand open because I stand secure in the embrace of a love so sure I need no other defense, no other assurance. In every situation, I can live well and fulfill my destiny, no matter what. For I know nothing, neither pain, nor forgetfulness, nor unconsciousness, not even my death, can separate me from the love of God whose grace always, always, always opens me for more.

September 9—Waves of Meaning

This fall I took two walks on Ferry Beach in Saco, Maine, September 8th and 9th. On the first of those days I found the graph-like design of each wave inspiring. I imagined a graph showing the latest political polls, a pulse, or an analysis of demographics. I wondered what beach-graphs would look like if they plotted the strange undulations of meaning found in the reflections in this book, or the shaking of heaven and earth that concludes in the perfect peace of the new heaven and new earth. All at once the shakeup would undo us. Spread over time it is like a dance, or sanctification.

The next day the dawning light inspired me, giving me insights into how peace comes fresh, often packaged like manna—plenty enough for that day.

These days, like any day, have been inspiring because I looked for inspiration and God did not disappoint me. The conversation continues, and I believe it always will. It will come in waves of speaking and listening, thinking and dreaming, seeing and believing, action and rest. Knowing that the conversation may include interludes of silence, but the relationship with God still goes on, our anxiety gives way to anticipation, and stress relaxes into peace.

Waves of Meaning

I thank you, O barren sand,
That you give no meaning to the design
Of that line where water meets land.

And you, O ocean bound by the beach,
Thanks for expressing nothing
In the limit of each reach.

Is it God who presents you as a graph?
Or do I decide what I want you to mean,
Figuring it out on my own behalf?

I see possibilities, probabilities, and projections—
Data detailing designs for my dreams—
And what could come from current conditions,

But given how you recant so fast,
Holding the line for only a moment,
Should I expect any meaning to last?

It's tempting to see such rhythm meant for despair,
As if death loomed in its uneasy pulse,
Waiting for destruction another wave can't repair.

This pattern of peace leaves me perplexed,
Yet calmed by its cadence of fleeting flux,
I'm forever shaken to hope for what's next!

I thank you, O barren sand,
That you receive meaning in the design
Of that line where water meets land.

And you, O ocean bound by the beach,
Thanks for holding no one
To the limit of your reach.

The End

Made in the USA
Lexington, KY
15 October 2017